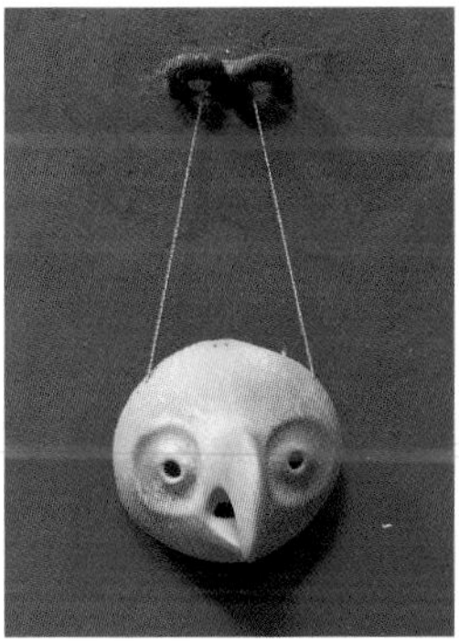

LIVING IN MEXICO

Photos and texts by BARBARA & RENÉ STOELTIE et al.
Edited by ANGELIKA TASCHEN

TASCHEN

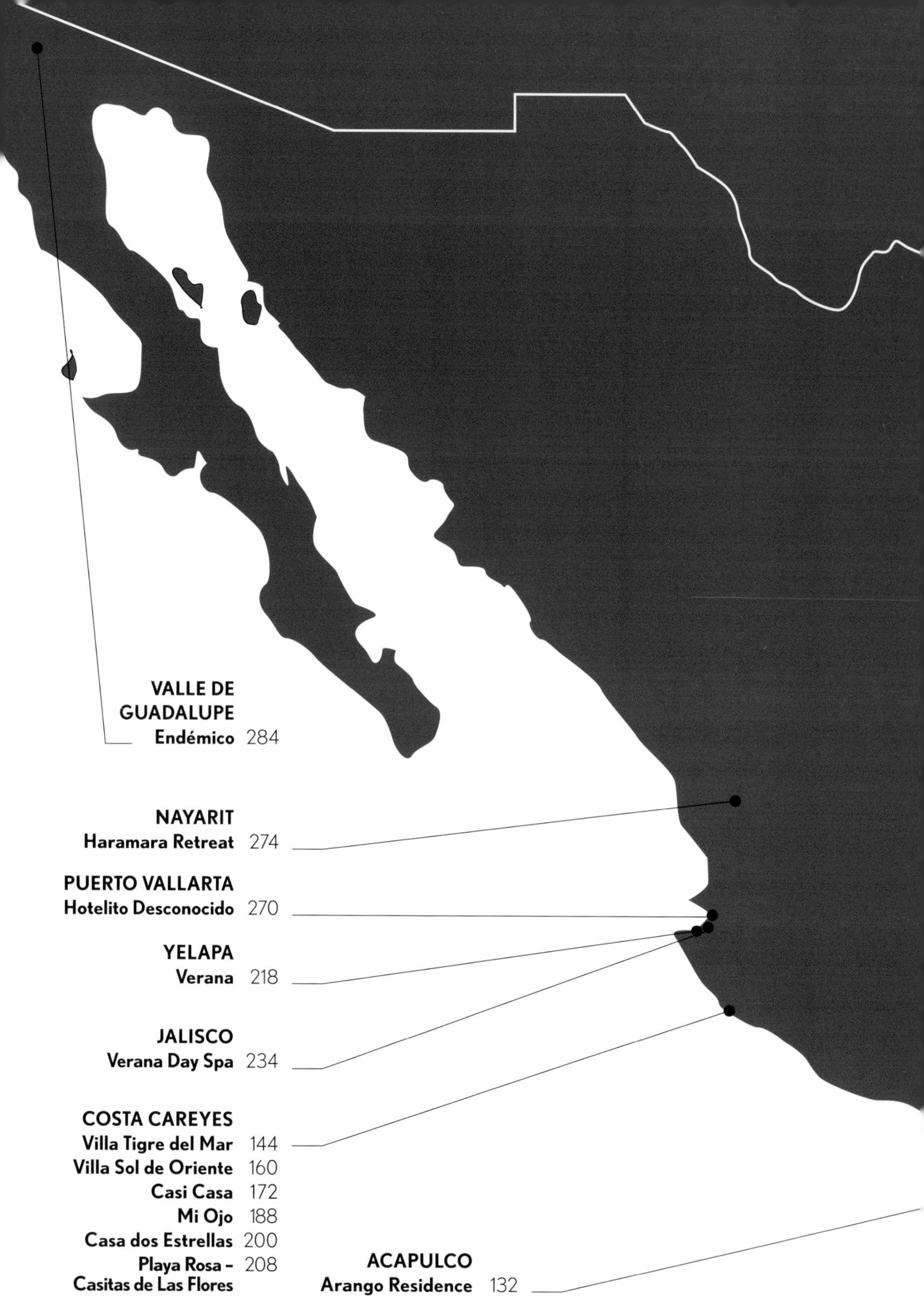

VALLE DE GUADALUPE
Endémico 284
NAYARIT
Haramara Retreat 274
PUERTO VALLARTA
Hotelito Desconocido 270
YELAPA
Verana 218
JALISCO
Verana Day Spa 234
COSTA CAREYES
Villa Tigre del Mar 144
Villa Sol de Oriente 160
Casi Casa 172
Mi Ojo 188
Casa dos Estrellas 200
Playa Rosa – Casitas de Las Flores 208
ACAPULCO
Arango Residence 132

TULUM
Amansala Eco Chic Resort 418
CACALCHÉN
A Converted Mayan House 406
ATOTONILCO
252 Hilltop Villa
MEXICO CITY
10 Casa Luis Barragán
24 A Converted Chapel
38 Condesa DF
56 P. & J. Senosiain House
MÉRIDA
A Collector's Passion 294
J. Powell & J. Ramos 302
Salvador R. Rios & Josefina L. Lagos 314
A Palapa House 328
Hacienda Xcumpich 338
Hacienda Poxila 354
Casa Cárdenas 366
CUERNAVACA
72 Casa de León
86 Casa de la Torre
104 V. M. Contreras
MORELOS
116 A Village House
YUCATÁN
Hacienda Petac 380
A Traditional Mayan House 398

CONTENTS

CONTENTS

CASA
LUIS BARRAGÁN

CASA LUIS BARRAGÁN

COLONIA TACUBAYA
MEXICO CITY

After Luis Barragán's death two books were found lying unfinished on his bedside table: Emily Brontë's "Wuthering Heights" and André Maurois' "A la recherche de Marcel Proust". This only goes to show that the spirit of Romanticism was never far from the legendary Mexican architect's heart – and that Barragán's work, all too often described as cerebral and minimalist, sprang from a lyrical mind. This "poet of stone", born in Guadalajara in 1902, began his career at the age of 23, establishing himself as one of the figureheads of Mexico's new architectural movement. Barragán, who was greatly influenced by the beauty of Italian towns and the gardens of El Generalife in Granada, went on to create his own distinctive constructions, which were marked by the sobriety of their style and used a typical palette of colours (bright yellows, Mexican pinks, electric blues and virginal whites). Barragán also experimented with a subtle play on volume, transforming his creations into three-dimensional Constructivist artworks. The architect's Mexican home, built in 1948 and where he died in 1988, reflects his love of visual calm and perfect volumes.

Nach seinem Tod fand man auf dem Nachttisch zwei Bücher, die er gerade zu lesen begonnen hatte: „Sturmhöhe" von Emily Brontë und „Auf den Spuren von Marcel Proust" von André Maurois. Die Romantik schien dem großen Architekten Luis Barragán nicht fremd zu sein, und man kann vermuten, dass auch sein Werk, das lange als intellektuell und minimalistisch galt, aus einer Gedankenwelt erwachsen ist, die lyrischen Empfindungen aufgeschlossen war. Dieser „Poet des Steins", 1902 in Guadalajara geboren, war schon mit 23 Jahren die Galionsfigur einer neuen Architektur. Die Schönheit italienischer Städte und die Gärten des Generalife in Granada beeinflussten Barrágans Werk, das sich durch die Einfachheit der Konstruktionen auszeichnet. Sein subtiles Spiel mit Räumen und seine Farbpalette aus leuchtendem Gelb, mexikanischem Rosa, kräftigem Hellblau und Schneeweiß ließen seine Gebäude wie dreidimensionale konstruktivistische Gemälde erscheinen. Barragáns Streben nach einem ruhigen Erscheinungsbild und der Perfektion des Raumes spiegeln sich in seinem 1948 in Mexico City gebauten Privathaus, in dem er 1988 starb.

Après sa mort, on a trouvé sur sa table de chevet deux livres dont il venait de commencer la lecture: « Les Hauts de Hurlevent », d'Emily Brontë et « À la recherche de Marcel Proust », d'André Maurois. Ceci tend à prouver que le romantisme n'était pas étranger au grand architecte Luis Barragán et que son œuvre, trop longtemps décrite comme cérébrale et minimaliste, est née d'un esprit sensible aux accents lyriques. Ce poète de la pierre, né à Guadalajara en 1902, s'est manifesté dès ses débuts à 23 ans comme l'une des figures de proue d'une architecture nouvelle. Influencé par la beauté des villes italiennes et par les jardins d'El Generalife à Grenade, Barragán s'est distingué par la sobriété de ses constructions, par sa palette de jaune vif, de rose mexicain, de bleu électrique et de blanc virginal et par ce jeu subtil de volumes qui transforment ses créations en tableaux constructivistes tridimensionnels. Sa maison privée à Mexico, construite en 1948 et où il est mort en 1988, reflète sa volonté de calme visuel et de perfection inégalée des volumes.

PP. 10–11 The vibrant shade of Mexican pink is omnipresent in Luis Barragán's architecture and forms a marvellous background to the luxuriant vegetation that often cascades over the walls of his courtyards. • Das lebhafte mexikanische Rosa, im architektonischen Werk Luis Barragáns allgegenwärtig, steht auf wunderbare Weise mit den blühenden Pflanzen im Einklang, die häufig die Mauern der großen Anwesen überwuchern. • Le « Rosa Mexicano » vibrant, omniprésent dans l'œuvre architecturale de Luis Barragán, sied à merveille à la végétation luxuriante qui envahit très souvent les murs des grandes propriétés.

P. 13 Bathed in shafts of sunlight, this terrace corner could have been inspired by a Constructivist painting. • In dem Streiflicht der Sonne wirkt diese Ecke der Terrasse wie ein konstruktivistisches Gemälde. • Un coin de la terrasse, caressé par le soleil, ressemble à un tableau constructiviste.

← Secluded behind high stone parapets, this private terrace with its vivid pink wall and flamboyant cascades of bougainvillea is a magical sight. • Mit ihrer Wand in leuchtendem Rosa und den Kaskaden von Bougainvillea bietet die von hohen Mauern geschützte Terrasse einen bezaubernden Anblick. • Protégée par de hauts murs, la terrasse enchante le regard avec son mur rose vif et ses cascades de bougainvillées.

← The architect has created a fireplace in the wall separating the entrance hall from the studio. • Zwischen Eingangsbereich und Studio hat der Architekt einen Kamin in die Wand eingelassen. • L'architecte a intégré une cheminée dans le mur qui sépare l'entrée du studio.

↑ The entrance hall is stunning in its simplicity. A bare pink wall together with the pure lines of the staircase and simple furniture create an atmosphere of peace and calm. • Der Eingangsraum überrascht: Die rosafarbene Wand, eine schlichte Treppe und streng geometrische Möbel schaffen ein ruhiges Ambiente. • Le hall d'entrée est surprenant. Un mur rose, un escalier épuré et des meubles aux lignes sévères créent une ambiance très calme.

→ Luis Barragán had an impeccable eye for colour and this is reflected throughout in immaculately painted walls, an interior shutter in Mexican pink, a ceiling punctuated with bright yellow beams and the furniture set off by pale wooden floorboards. • Luis Barragáns außergewöhnliches Gespür für Farbgestaltung zeigt sich in den sauber gestrichenen Wänden, den kräftiggelben Balken der Zimmerdecke, dem Fensterrollo in mexikanischem Rosa sowie in den Möbeln und dem hellen Parkett. • Des murs immaculés, un plafond embelli par le rythme des poutres jaune vif, un volet intérieur rose mexicain, des meubles et un parquet blond témoignent des qualités exceptionnelles de coloriste de Luis Barragán.

↑ → The pure, simple lines of the staircase leading up to the guest bedroom. • Die Treppe zum Obergeschoss überzeugt durch klare Formen. • L'escalier qui monte vers une chambre d'amis séduit par la pureté de ses lignes.

← Luis Barragán's bedroom is a study in austerity, the only décorbeing a crucifix and a small collection of objets d'art that reflects the Mexican architect's pure, ascetic tastes. • Kruzifix und wenige Kunstobjekte in Barragáns schlichtem Schlafzimmer zeugen von puristischem Geschmack. • Dans la chambre de Barragán, dépouillée à l'extrême, le crucifix et les objets d'art témoignent de la rigueur chère à l'architecte.

A CONVERTED CHAPEL

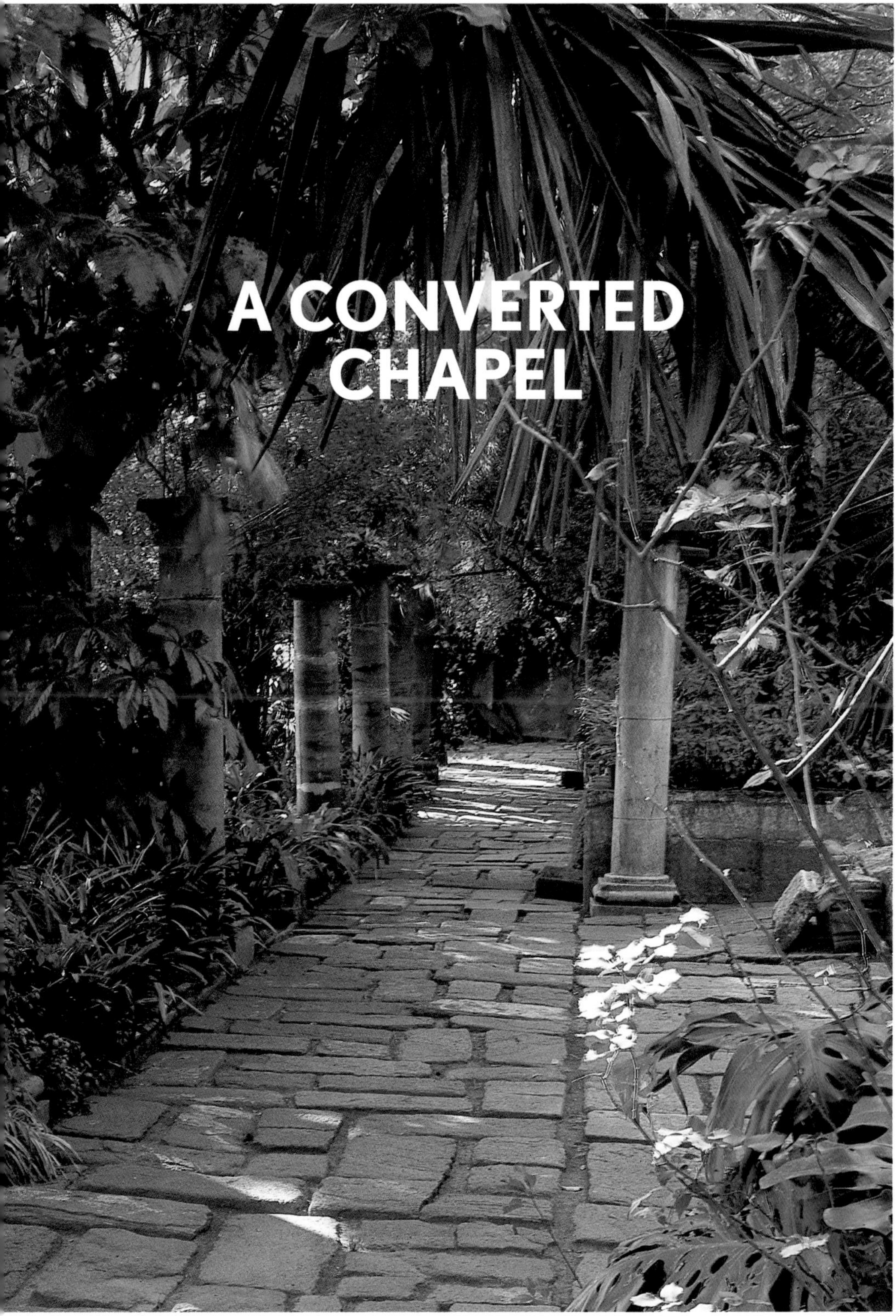

A CONVERTED CHAPEL

SERGIO BERGER
MEXICO CITY

Sergio Berger is young, handsome and at the height of professional success after opening "Ivory", his third restaurant in the Mexican capital. Despite his lightning rise to fame, Sergio has retained the natural modesty and reserve common to romantic souls such as himself. These aspects of the restaurant owner's character led him to make a rather unusual choice of home, setting himself up in a 16th-century chapel. But Sergio never had any intention of living in a shrine, surrounded by burning candles and the reproving stares of plaster saints. While the chapel's original frescoes and Baroque Hispanic altar with its ornate gilt surrounds have been retained, this historical décor starkly contrasts with the modern minimalist architecture and the owner's eclectic tastes. His collection of contemporary art, African artworks and an impressive variety of furniture sets up an interesting visual tension between itself and the religious surroundings. In short, Sergio Berger brings 21st-century style and a sense of fun to chapel life.

Er ist jung und gut aussehend und hat gerade mit „Ivory" sein drittes Restaurant in der mexikanischen Hauptstadt eröffnet. Dabei hat sich Sergio Berger trotz seines blendenden Erfolgs die Bescheidenheit und Zurückhaltung eines sensiblen Naturells bewahrt. Für diesen Charakterzug spricht auch die ungewöhnliche Entscheidung, sich in einer Kapelle aus dem 16. Jahrhundert einzurichten. Allerdings stand ihm nicht der Sinn danach, seine Tage in einer Leichenhalle zu verbringen, umringt von Kerzen und farbigen Heiligenfiguren aus Gips, die ihn missbilligend anblicken könnten. Deshalb ließ der Junggastronom nur den reich verzierten und vergoldeten hispanischen Barockaltar sowie die Fresken unangetastet. Der Kontrast von historischen Dekorationen, karger Architektur und Sergios eklektizistischem Geschmack, in dem zeitgenössische und afrikanische Kunst sich mit Möbeln aller Stilrichtungen verbindet, lässt natürlich eine große visuelle Spannung entstehen. In einer Kapelle leben, ja, aber mit der Einstellung des 21. Jahrhunderts und ohne sich dabei allzu ernst zu nehmen.

Il est jeune et beau et vient d'ouvrir son troisième restaurant baptisé « Ivory » dans la capitale mexicaine. En dépit de son succès foudroyant, Sergio Berger a su préserver une modestie et une timidité qui sont le propre des êtres romantiques. D'ailleurs, son choix singulier de s'installer dans une chapelle du 16e siècle ne fait qu'accentuer cet aspect de son caractère. Néanmoins, Sergio n'avait aucune envie de passer ses journées dans une ambiance de chapelle ardente, entouré de cierges et de saints en plâtre polychrome déplorant son intrusion et le fixant d'un air réprobateur. Le jeune restaurateur a gardé l'autel hispanique baroque lourdement doré et ornementé et n'a pas touché aux fresques. Le contraste entre les décorations d'époque, l'architecture sévère et le goût éclectique de Sergio qui combine l'art contemporain, l'art africain et les meubles en tout genre, crée bien sûr une grande tension visuelle. D'accord pour vivre dans une chapelle, mais dans l'esprit du 21e siècle et sans trop se prendre au sérieux.

PP. 24–25 Tucked away in the heart of town, this tranquil enclave with its centuries-old walled gardens stands as an ode to rural life. • Diese mitten in der Stadt gelegene, friedliche Enklave mit ihren jahrhundertealten, ummauerten Gärten wirkt wie der Inbegriff ländlichen Lebens. • Au cœur de la ville, cette enclave paisible avec ses jardins murés vieux de plusieurs siècles fait l'éloge de la vie rurale.

P. 27 The impressive carved wooden door of the former chapel is original and dates from the 16th-century. • Die eindrucksvolle geschnitzte Holztür der alten Kapelle ist originalgetreu erhalten und stammt aus dem 16. Jahrhundert. • L'imposante porte en bois sculpté de l'ancienne chapelle est authentique et date du seizième siècle.

← ↑ Sergio has created a guest room in the mezzanine complete with an inviting couch piled high with Indian cushions. The hand of Buddha is carved out of wood. • Im Zwischengeschoss hat Sergio ein Gästezimmer mit einem Sofa eingerichtet, auf dem mehrere aus Indien mitgebrachte Kissen liegen. Die Hand des Buddha ist aus Holz. • Sergio a créé une chambre d'amis dans l'entresol en y installant un lit de repos dissimulé sous un amoncellement de coussins rapportés d'Inde. La main de Bouddha est en bois sculpté.

↑ The vivid colours of Ray Smith's painting blend with the kaleidoscopic assortment of furniture in the living room (converted from its former existence as a chapel). • Im Wohnzimmer der früheren Kapelle passt das farbenfrohe Gemälde von Ray Smith perfekt zu den Möbeln der unterschiedlichen Stilrichtungen. • Le tableau aux vives couleurs de Ray Smith se marie avec bonheur aux meubles hétéroclites dans le séjour, une ancienne chapelle.

→ A brightly coloured budgerigar; detail of a painting by Ray Smith. • Ein hübscher Wellensittich, Ausschnitt aus einem Gemälde von Ray Smith. • Une jolie perruche, détail d'un tableau signé Ray Smith.

← An antique wooden reredos, hand-painted and embellished with exquisite gilt decoration, is the central feature in the living room. • Den Blickfang im Wohnzimmer bildet die historische Altarrückwand aus bemaltem und vergoldetem Holz. • L'ancien retable en bois peint et doré domine le séjour.

↑ Sergio retained the delicate frescoes adorning the chapel walls. • Den zarten Freskenschmuck der Kapelle hat Sergio erhalten. • Sergio a conservé les fresques délicates qui ornent les murs de la chapelle.

PP. 34–35 In choosing the colours for his bedroom, Sergio Berger took his inspiration from natural shades, such as sand and wood. The chest at the foot of the bed and the doors are beautiful antiques. • Was die Wahl der Farben für sein Schlafzimmer betrifft, hat sich Sergio Berger zwanglos von natürlichen, sand- oder holzfarbenen Tönen inspirieren lassen. Die Truhe am Fußende des Bettes und die Türen sind aus der gleichen Epoche. • Pour le choix des couleurs de sa chambre à coucher, Sergio Berger s'est inspiré librement des teintes naturelles comme le sable et le bois. Le coffret au pied du lit et les portes sont d'époque.

↑ Trio: decorative tassels. • Dreierlei: schmückende Kordeln. • Trio : ravissantes cordelettes.

→ On the side of the bathtub, the elegant silhouette of a very handsome African mask. • Die sehr schöne, elegant konturierte afrikanische Maske auf dem Rand der Badewanne ist ein Blickfang. • Sur le rebord de la baignoire, on découvre la silhouette élégante d'un très beau masque africain.

CONDESA DF

CONDESA DF

MEXICO CITY

Situated in the heart of Mexico City is the Condesa DF, one of the metropolis' few chic hotels. Originally built in 1928 as an apartment block, this triangular building was converted into a hip hotel in 2005 by architect Javier Sánchez and star interior designer India Mahdavi of Paris. The ethos isn't just about style, however; the hotel has identified QIPs ("Quiet Important People") as their key target group. Here, these aficionados of good but unintrusive service benefit from free Wi-Fi Internet access in surroundings entirely free from brash extravagance. At dusk, guests can enjoy the hotel's roof terrace (quietly, of course) and admire the fabulous views across the largely undesigned expanses of Mexico City.

Mitten in der lebhaften Metropole Mexico City liegt mit dem Condesa DF eines der wenigen urbanen, schicken Hotels der Stadt. Schon 1928 wurde dieses Gebäude mit dreieckigem Grundriss als Apartmentblock entworfen; 2005 verwandelten es der Architekt Javier Sánchez und die meisterhafte Pariser Innenraumdesignerin India Mahdavi in eine hippe Adresse. Es geht aber nicht nur um schickes Design, schließlich hat man hier die QIPs (Quiet Important People) als neue Zielgruppe entdeckt. Diesen Liebhabern des diskreten, guten Services soll der Aufenthalt etwa mit freiem WLAN so angenehm wie möglich gemacht werden – protzige Extravaganz bleibt draußen. Wenn es dämmert, wird die Dachterrasse zum Hotspot, dank eines wunderbaren Blicks über das komplett undesignte Mexico City. Aber nicht vergessen: „Quiet, please!"

En plein cœur de la trépidante métropole de Mexico se trouve l'un des rares hôtels de style urbain chic de la ville. Dès sa conception en 1928, ce bâtiment de forme triangulaire avait été pensé comme un immeuble collectif. En 2005, l'architecte Javier Sánchez et la décoratrice d'intérieur parisienne India Mahdavi en ont fait une adresse branchée. Le design chic n'est pas forcément l'essentiel ici. On cible en effet une nouvelle clientèle, les QIP (Quiet Important People). Des équipements très utiles, comme le libre accès à Internet en WiFi, agrémentent au mieux le séjour de ces adeptes du service discret et de qualité – frimeurs s'abstenir. Quand la nuit tombe, on vient bien sûr profiter du toit-terrasse (en respectant le calme exigé !), avec une vue splendide sur un Mexico resté dans son jus.

PP. 38–39 Guests on the triangular terrace of the Hotel Condesa DF can enjoy a marvellous view of the abundant plant-life around them. • Von der dreieckigen Terrasse oben auf dem Hotel Condesa DF in Mexiko-Stadt bietet sich den Gästen ein freier Blick auf die üppige Vegetation der Umgebung. • De la terrasse triangulaire au sommet de l'Hôtel Condesa DF, les hôtes peuvent profiter d'une vue imprenable sur la végétation abondante des alentours.

P. 41 The architect Javier Sánchez has contrived a perfect combination of a resolutely contemporary style and the air of old-world distinction belonging to a classic building of the late 1920s. • Dem Architekten Javier Sánchez ist eine ideale Verbindung von zeitgenössischer Architektur und dem vornehmen Stil eines 1928 entstandenen Gebäudes gelungen. • L'architecte Javier Sánchez a réussi un mariage parfait entre une architecture résolument contemporaine et l'allure distinguée d'un bâtiment classique né en 1928.

← A bird's-eye view of the hotel patio from the roof-terrace. The walls of the spectacular triangular courtyard are covered in brise-soleils to protect the rooms from the sun. • Von der Terrasse aus schweift der Blick hinab in den Patio des Hotels. Die Wände des eindrucksvollen dreieckigen Innenhofs sind mit zahlreichen Fensterläden versehen, die den Ort vor den Sonnenstrahlen schützen. • De la terrasse, on a une vue plongeante sur le patio de l'hôtel. Les parois de la spectaculaire cour triangulaire s'habillent d'une multitude de volets qui protègent l'endroit des rayons de soleil.

→ India Mahdavi designed all the hotel's furniture and her kidney-shaped table on the terrace is inspired by the "boomerang" shapes typical of the 1950s. • India Mahdavi hat die komplette Ausstattung des Hotels entworfen. Der nierenförmige Tisch, dem auf der Terrasse ein wichtiger Platz zugewiesen wurde, ist nach den typischen „Bumerang"-Formen der 1950er Jahre gestaltet. • India Mahdavi a crée tout le mobilier de l'hôtel. La table en forme de rognon qui occupe une place importante sur la terrasse s'inspire des formes « boomerang » typiques des années 1950.

PP. 46–47 The designer decorated the hotel bar with her own creations and the imposing forms of her "Bishop" bar-stools stand out. • Die Designerin hat die Bar des Hotels mit originellen Kreationen ausgestattet. Die Rundungen ihrer auffälligen „Bishop"-Hocker zum Beispiel sind nicht zu übersehen. • La designer a décoré le bar de l'hôtel avec ses créations originales : on y remarque d'emblée la présence dominante et les rondeurs de ses tabourets « Bishop ».

← Mahdavi sought something like Barragán's minimalism in the exemplary austerity of her decorations for the Condesa DF. The wood panelling of the walls immediately catches the eye. • Bei der Ausstattung des Condesa DF hat Mahdavi versucht, sich dem minimalistischen schöpferischen Geist Barragáns mit mustergültiger Einfachheit zu nähern. Die mit Holz ausgekleideten Wände fallen ins Auge. • Mahdavi a cherché à s'approcher de l'esprit minimal de Barragàn en décorant le Condesa DF avec un dépouillement exemplaire. Les parois habillées de bois accrochent tout de suite le regard.

↑ Here everything revolves around the magnificent white table designed by Mahdavi. The pastel colour of the walls imparts a typical 1960s atmosphere. • Hier steht der herrliche, für die Handschrift der Designerin typische weiße Tisch im Mittelpunkt. Die Pastellfarbe der Wände verleiht dem Ort eine typische Sechzigerjahre-Atmosphäre. • Ici tout évolue autour de la magnifique table blanche qui porte la signature de la designer. La couleur pastel des murs plonge l'endroit dans une ambiance typiquement « sixties ».

↑ Who has not dreamed of a room open on every side? In the penthouse of the hotel, the architect has realized this dream; one has only to open the curtains for the beneficent sunlight to flood into the room. • Wer träumt nicht von einem licht- und luftdurchfluteten Zimmer? Auf dem Dachgeschoss des Hotels ist es dem Architekten gelungen, diesen Traum zu verwirklichen. Man braucht bloß die Vorhänge beiseite zu ziehen, und schon kann man die wohltuenden Strahlen der Sonne genießen. • Qui n'a pas rêvé d'une chambre ouverte à tous les vents ? Au sommet de l'hôtel, l'architecte a réussi à réaliser ce rêve et on n'a qu'à écarter les rideaux pour profiter des rayons de soleil bienfaisants.

↗ White curtains, a comfortable sofa and designer furniture: in this "eagle's nest" opening directly onto the terrace, the deep upholstery is an invitation to indolence. • Weiße Vorhänge, ein bequemes Sofa und Designermöbel: Das luxuriöse Ambiente dieser wie ein Adlerhorst anmutenden Suite, die sich direkt auf eine Terrasse öffnet, lädt buchstäblich zur Entspannung ein. • Des rideaux blancs, un canapé confortable et du mobilier design : dans cette suite en « nid d'aigle » qui s'ouvre directement sur la terrasse, l'ambiance feutrée invite à la paresse.

← The pure, geometrical design of these walls panelled with different exotic woods is not unlike the severe patterning of Japanese "Shoji" screens. • Die klare und geometrische Gestaltung der mit unterschiedlichen exotischen Hölzern ausgekleideten Wände dieses Zimmers lässt an den strengen Stil der japanischen „Shoji"-Paravents denken. • Dans cette chambre le dessin pur et géométrique des parois habillées de différents bois exotiques n'est pas sans rappeler le graphisme sévère des paravents « shoji » japonais.

↑ The mild climate allowed the architect to include large bay-windows; the guests can enjoy life in the open air while remaining in the comfort of their suite. • Das milde Klima erlaubte es dem Architekten, große verglaste Fenster einzubauen, die es den Gästen ermöglichen, das Leben draußen an der frischen Luft zu verfolgen, ohne das komfortable Ambiente ihrer Suite zu verlassen. • La douceur du climat a permis à l'architecte d'introduire de grandes baies vitrées qui permettent aux hôtes de profiter au maximum de la vie au grand air tout en restant confortablement à l'intérieur de leur suite.

↑ With its baldachin supporting long white curtains, the bathtub is like a sumptuous à la polonaise bed. • Mit ihrem von langen, weißen Vorhängen umkränzten Baldachin ähnelt die Badewanne einem prächtigen „Lit à la polonaise", einem Himmelbett, das in der ersten Hälfte des 18. Jahrhunderts in Mode kam. • Avec son baldaquin habillé de longs rideaux blancs, la baignoire ressemble à un lit « à la polonaise » somptueux.

→ In the bathroom, the basin echoes the form of the "Bishop" stool by the hotel's decorator, Mahdavi. • Das Waschbecken im Badezimmer erinnert an die Formen der von der Designerin geschaffenen „Bishop"-Hocker. • Dans la salle de bains, le lavabo fait écho à la forme du tabouret « Bishop » créé par la décoratrice.

PALOMA & JAVIER SENOSIAIN HOUSE

PALOMA & JAVIER SENOSIAIN HOUSE

MEXICO CITY, VISTA DEL VALLE

In the tradition of the biomorphic or organic architecture of Bruce Goff, Paolo Soleri and Frank Lloyd Wright as well as Antonio Gaudí, Senosiain looked to seashells, skulls and sponges for formal inspiration for the ferro-cement construction of his own house, which is in the shape of a shark.

In der Tradition großer biomorpher oder organischer Architektur wie von Bruce Goff, Paolo Soleri, Frank Lloyd Wright und Antoni Gaudí suchte Senosiain beim Bau seines eigenen Hauses – eine Ferrozement-Konstruktion in Form eines Hais – formale Inspiration bei Muscheln, Schädeln und Schwämmen.

Se situant dans la tradition de l'architecture biomorphique ou organique à l'instar de Bruce Goff, Paolo Soleri, Frank Lloyd Wright ou encore Antoni Gaudí, Senosiain s'est inspiré de coquillages, de crânes et d'éponges pour créer sa demeure en béton armé reprenant la forme d'un requin.

PP. 56–57 Paloma and Javier Senosiain's extraordinary house emerges from the verdant hillside in an array of organic shapes evocative of fishes and seashells. • Der ungewöhnliche Wohnsitz von Paloma und Javier Senosiain ragt mit seinen organischen Formen, die an Fische und Muscheln erinnern, aus dem grünen Hügel hervor. • La demeure extraordinaire de Paloma et Javier Senosiain émerge de la colline verdoyante en prenant des formes organiques qui font penser à celles des poissons et des coquillages.

P. 59 Like some astonishing excrescence, the sinuous house rests gently on vast expanses of lawn. • Sanft und wie eine merkwürdige Wucherung schmiegt sich das gewundene Haus an eine weitläufige Rasenlandschaft an. • Telle une excroissance bizarre, la maison sinueuse se couche mollement sur une vaste étendue de gazon.

PP. 60–61 Dense vegetation, dominated by the vivid colour of a bougainvillea cascade, surrounds the impressive gateway that leads to this futuristic domain. • Eine dichte, von der explosiven Farbe einer Bougainvillea-Kaskade dominierte Vegetation überwuchert das imposante Tor, das den Eingang zu der futuristischen Bleibe bildet. • Une végétation dense, dominée par la couleur explosive d'une cascade de bougainvillées, envahit l'imposante porte qui mène à ce domaine futuriste.

← Like the "mouths" of the Paris Métro, which Dalí likened to predatory mantids, the entrance to the house is like the mouth of a giant carnivorous plant ready to engulf all those who dare to enter. • Ebenso wie die von Dalí „Friss mich" getauften Eingänge der Pariser Métro ähnelt auch der Hauseingang dem Maul einer riesigen, fleischfressenden Pflanze, allzeit bereit, jeden, der es wagt einzutreten, zu verschlingen. • Tout comme les bouches de métro parisiens baptisées « mange-moi » par Dali, l'entrée de la maison ressemble à la bouche d'une gigantesque plante carnivore prête à happer tout ceux qui ont l'audace d' y entrer.

↑ Seen from outside, the great bay window of the living room bears an alarming resemblance to the eye of a Cyclops. The vegetation over the bay forms a luxuriant eyebrow. • Von außen betrachtet überrascht das große Fenster des Wohnzimmers durch seine beunruhigende Ähnlichkeit mit dem riesigen Auge eines Zyklopen. Die Pflanzen, die das Fenster bekrönen, wirken dabei wie der Bogen einer Augenbraue. • Vue de l'extérieur, la grande baie vitrée du séjour surprend par sa ressemblance inquiétante avec l'œil gigantesque d'un cyclope. La végétation qui couronne la baie fait office d'arcade sourcilière.

PP. 64–65 Organic form in all its splendour, the impressive space of the living room undulates and meanders like a magnificent Art Nouveau jewel. The seat in the form of a hand is a major work by the Mexican sculptor Pedro Friedeberg (b. 1936). • Die gewellten und schlängelnden Formen des in seiner ganzen Pracht und in beeindruckenden Ausmaßen organisch gestalteten Wohnzimmers breiten sich aus wie die eines herrlichen Art-nouveau-Juwels. Der an der Form einer Hand orientierte Sitz ist ein bedeutendes Werk des mexikanischen Bildhauers Pedro Friedeberg (*1936). • Organique dans toute sa splendeur, le volume impressionnant du séjour ondule et serpentine tel un magnifique bijou Art Nouveau. Le siège qui imite la forme d'une main est une œuvre majeure du sculpteur mexicain Pedro Friedeberg (né en 1936).

← The interior is a stark challenge to angular architecture; one is as if transported to the heart of a giant mollusc. • Das Innere ist eine wahre Kampfansage an eine Architektur mit Ecken und Winkeln. Man hat den Eindruck, sich im Leib eines gigantischen Weichtiers zu befinden. • L'intérieur est un véritable défi à l'architecture angulaire et on a l'impression de se trouver au cœur d'un gigantesque mollusque.

↑ A little cell has been crafted in the wall, with its own skylight, a mattress and a "mobile" in the spirit of Calder. • Eine Aushöhlung der Wand wurde mit einem Lichtschacht versehen, einer Matratze ausgestattet und einem Mobile im Stile Calders ausgeschmückt. • Creusée dans un mur, une alvéole a été équipée d'une lucarne et d'un matelas et agrémentée d'un « mobile » dans l'esprit de Calder.

PP. 68–69 In Paloma and Javier's extraordinary house, every object obeys the dictates of organic form. • Auch die Alltagsobjekte im Hause von Paloma und Javier haben sich dem organischen Formenkanon unterzuordnen. • Dans la demeure extraordinaire de Paloma et Javier, les objets familiers obéissent à la dictature des formes organiques.

↑ Despite the long, elegant lines of the bookshelves, the bedroom resembles nothing so much as the volute interior of a vast snail-shell. • Trotz eines lang gestreckten Bücherregals wirkt das Schlafzimmer eher wie ein Gehäuse einer riesigen Schnecke. • Malgré la présence d'une bibliothèque longiligne, le volume de chambre à coucher ressemble comme une goutte d'eau à la coquille d'un escargot gigantesque .

→ It is difficult to avoid the idea that this house is a petrified organism and that one is living in the entrails of an immense and fantastical life form. • Es ist schwer, sich von der Vorstellung zu befreien, dass dieses Haus ein versteinerter Organismus sein könnte, in dem man lebt, als würde man sich in den Eingeweiden eines enormen phantastischen Fabelwesens bewegen. • Il est difficile de se défaire de l'idée que cette maison est un organisme pétrifié et qu'on y vit comme si on évoluait dans les entrailles d'un immense animal fantastique.

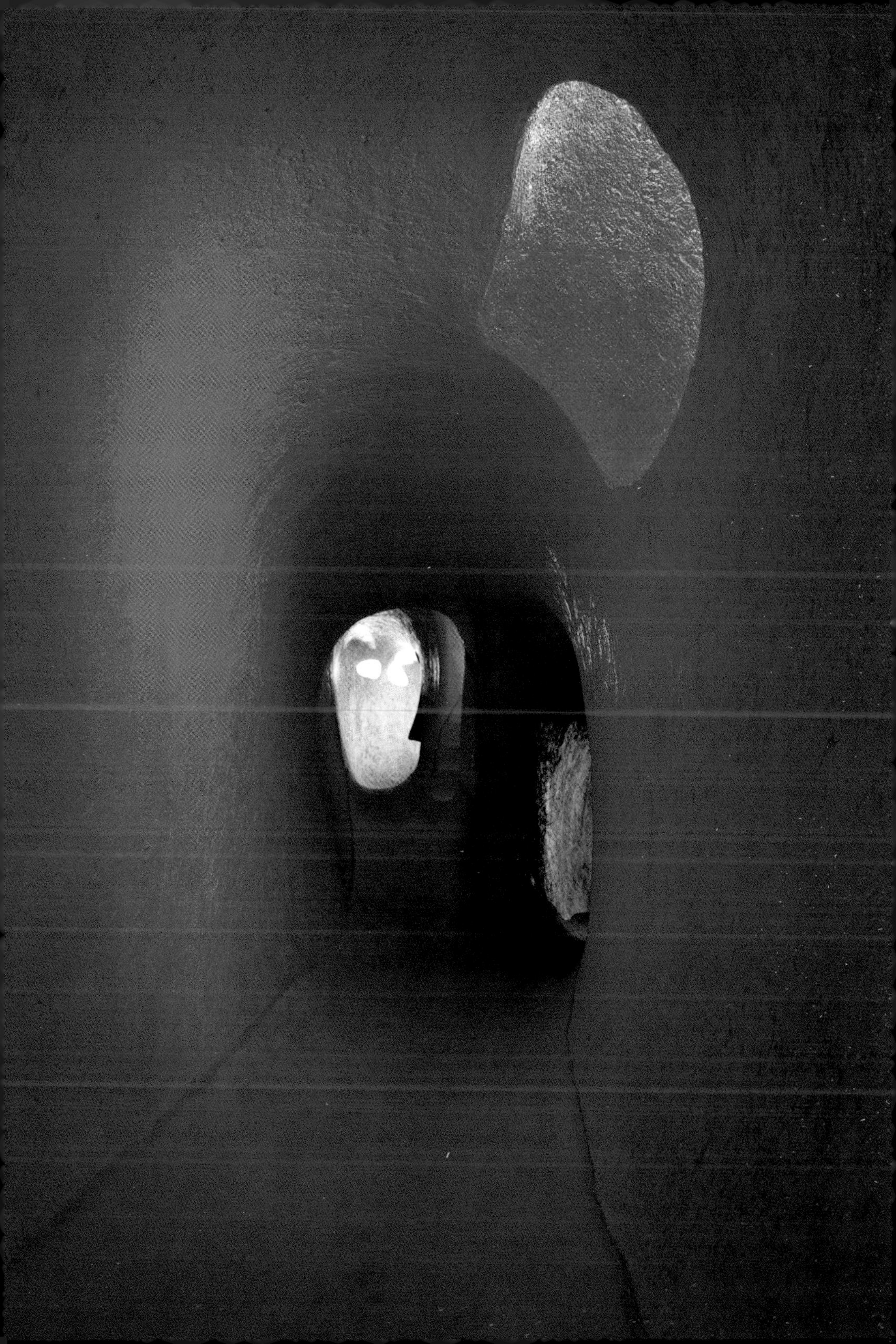

CASA DE LEÓN

CASA DE LEÓN

EVELYN LAMBERT
CUERNAVACA

With her large-framed glasses and hair pulled back into a neat platinum chignon, Evelyn Lambert appeared to have discovered the secret of eternal youth. At the age of 97, she was still fired by remarkable energy and a tireless curiosity about the world around her and took a keen interest in the arts, especially 20th-century art, which she had admired, defended and collected with the passion of a true connoisseur. Evelyn, American by birth, discovered art through direct contact with artists themselves and she spent much of her life mixing with the greatest of them. Her refined sense of aesthetics led her to live in a splendid villa in Veneto before she settled in the heart of Cuernavaca in this magnificent 17th-century house in the late 1980s. These days the Casa de León, a former brothel known as the Casa del Gato (House of the Cat), still houses a superb collection of paintings, sculptures, antiques and objets d'art arranged according to Evelyn's original eye for décor. Sadly, the mistress of the Casa de León has passed away, leaving behind a wide circle of friends and admirers.

Evelyn Lambert schien dem Geheimnis ewiger Jugend auf die Spur gekommen zu sein: Noch mit 97 Jahren legte sie eine beachtliche Energie an den Tag und verfolgte mit großem Interesse und Neugier das Geschehen auf dieser Welt, insbesondere in Bezug auf die Kunst. Mit Leidenschaft unterstützte und sammelte sie die von ihr bewunderte Kunst des 20. Jahrhunderts. Die gebürtige Amerikanerin, die eine riesige Brille und einen kleinen platinfarbenen Haarknoten trug, war über die Künstler zur Kunst gestoßen. Man konnte sie nur bewundern, diese Frau, die mit den Großen Umgang hatte und aus Liebe zum Schönen beschloss, sich in einer prächtigen Villa im Veneto niederzulassen, ehe sie Ende der 1980er Jahre in ein wunderbares Haus im Herzen von Cuernavaca zog. Die Casa de León, die einmal Casa del Gato (Haus der Katze) hieß und ein Bordell war, beherbergt heute immer noch Gemälde, Skulpturen, Objekte und Antiquitäten, allesamt mit einer Originalität angeordnet, die von Evelyns Talent zum Inszenieren zeugt. Mit fast 100 Jahren ist die Hausherrin nun verstorben. Sie verstand bis zuletzt, ihre Freunde und Bewunderer zu bezaubern.

Evelyn Lambert semblait avoir découvert le secret de la jeunesse éternelle. À 97 ans, elle faisait encore preuve d'une énergie remarquable et d'une curiosité inlassable pour tout ce qui existe et surtout les arts – en particulier l'art du 20e siècle qu'elle n'a jamais cessé d'admirer, de défendre et de collectionner avec passion. Américaine de naissance, Evelyn, immenses lunettes et petit chignon platine, avait découvert l'art à travers les artistes. Impossible de ne pas admirer cette femme qui côtoyait les grands et qui choisit, par amour du beau, de vivre dans une superbe villa du Veneto, avant de s'installer à la fin des années 1980 dans une magnifique demeure du 17e siècle au cœur de Cuernavaca. Aujourd'hui la Casa de León, qui s'appelait jadis la Casa del Gato (la maison du chat) et était une maison close, abrite toujours les tableaux, les sculptures, les objets et les antiquités disposés avec une originalité qui révèle le talent d'Evelyn pour la mise en scène. Hélas, à l'approche de ses cent printemps, la maîtresse des lieux s'est éteinte. Mais elle continue toujours d'enchanter ses amis et ses admirateurs.

PP. 72–73 An elegant fountain, inspired by those found in Italian Renaissance gardens, supplies water to the swimming pool in the lower half of the garden. • Das im unteren Teil des Gartens gelegene Schwimmbecken wird von einer eleganten Fontäne gespeist, die den Brunnen italienischer Renaissancegärten nachempfunden ist. • La piscine, située dans la partie basse du jardin, est alimentée en eau par une fontaine élégante inspirée de celles des jardins de la Renaissance italienne.

P. 75 Standing by the fountain's basin, visitors have a stunning view of the garden and its lush vegetation. • Vom Brunnenbecken aus eröffnet sich eine wunderbare Aussicht auf den üppig wuchernden Garten. • Du bassin de la fontaine, on a une vue magnifique sur le jardin luxuriant.

→ The garden of the Casa de León is an oasis of greenery, its tranquillity broken only by birdsong and the gentle play of fountains • Der Garten der Casa de León ist eine grüne Oase, in der nur das Plätschern der Springbrunnen und die Vögel zu hören sind • Le jardin de la Casa de León est une oasis de verdure où l'on n'entend que le murmure des fontaines et le chant des oiseaux.

↑ In the hallway of the late Evelyn Lambert's house, an exotic statue in gilded bronze keeps guard over the stairs that lead up to the living room. • Im Eingangsbereich des Hauses von Evelyn Lambert wacht eine exotische Statue aus vergoldeter Bronze auf den Stufen, die den Zugang zum Wohnzimmer gewähren. • Dans l'entrée de la maison de feu Evelyn Lambert, une statue exotique en bronze doré montait la garde sur les marches qui donnaient accès au séjour.

→ A sculpture by Garth Evans from 1968 dominates the stairwell decorated with eye-catching mosaics and the gentle curve of a banister. • Eine Garth-Evans-Skulptur von 1968 beherrscht das Treppenhaus mit seinen auffallenden Mosaiken und dem geschwungenen Handlauf. • Une sculpture de Garth Evans, de 1968, domine la cage d'escalier avec ses mosaïques et sa rampe aux lignes souples.

← In her decorative schemes, Evelyn contrived the most audacious and unexpected combinations. Her patio, which was also her office, displays rattan furniture and a Tunisian birdcage alongside a contemporary painting. • Was die Ausstattung anbelangt, ließ sich Evelyn auf kühne und völlig unvermutete Wagnisse ein. In ihrem Patio, der zugleich als Büro diente, gelang ihr die Kombination traditioneller Korbmöbel mit einem tunesischen Vogelkäfig und einem zeitgenössischen Tisch. • En matière de décoration, Evelyn osait des mélanges audacieux et totalement inattendus. Dans son patio qui faisait aussi office de bureau, elle réussit à marier un mobilier en rotin traditionnel avec une cage à oiseaux tunisienne et un tableau contemporain.

↑ The painting by Jeremy Moon, "Indian Journey", offsets the colourful tones of a carved wooden fruit bowl. • Das Gemälde von Jeremy Moon, „Indian Journey", passt sehr schön zu einer bunten Fruchtschale aus geschnitztem Holz. • Le tableau signé Jeremy Moon, « Indian Journey », s'harmonise avec une coupe à fruits en bois sculpté polychrome.

↑ Gifted with exceptional aesthetic taste and a "sense of the dramatic", Evelyn Lambert had transferred the décor of her now legendary Italian villa near Vicenza to her Mexican home in Cuernavaca. Francis Celentano's 1963 painting above the sofa, entitled "December 30", hangs alongside Venetian Blackamoors. • Mit ihrem ausgeprägten „Sinn für Dramatik" übertrug Evelyn die berühmte Einrichtung ihrer bei Vicenza gelegenen italienischen Villa in ihr mexikanisches Haus. Das Bild über dem Sofa mit dem Titel „December 30" hat Francis Celentano 1963 gemalt. Hier wird es kombiniert mit venezianischen Mohrenfigur-Leuchtern. • Avec son sens exceptionnel du « dramatique », Evelyn transposa la décoration désormais célèbre de sa villa italienne située près de Vicence dans sa maison mexicaine. Le tableau au-dessus du canapé date de 1963. Il est signé Francis Celentano et s'intitule « December 30 ». Il côtoie ici des Blackamoors vénitiens.

→ The hand-painted wooden wardrobe in the loggia is a masterpiece of Italian Renaissance cabinetwork. • Der handbemalte Holzschrank der Loggia ist ein Stück Tischlerkunst aus der italienischen Renaissance. • L'armoire en bois peint de la loggia est un chef-d'œuvre d'ébénisterie de la Renaissance italienne.

IRELAND
ART AT THE TURN OF THE MILLENNIUM
Dallas Museum of Art
COUNTRY HOUSES of CENTRAL EUROPE

↑ Evelyn brought here certain period pieces from the Palladian villa that she used to own in the Veneto, and was particularly fond of this big 19th-century sofa in Second Empire style, which is as comfortable as it is handsome. • Aus ihrer alten Palladio-Villa im Veneto hatte sie einige alte Möbel mitgebracht. Das schöne, bequeme, im 19. Jahrhundert im Stil des Second Empire entworfene große Sofa hatte es ihr angetan. • De son ancienne villa palladienne dans le Veneto, elle avait gardé quelques meubles d'époque. Elle affectionnait particulièrement ce grand canapé 19 ième dans le style Napoléon III aussi beau que confortable.

→ In the living room, an ancient kneeling Buddha, covered in gold leaf, flanks a reproduction of the famous "Red-Blue" chair created in 1917 by the Dutch designer Gerrit Rietveld. • Im Wohnzimmer leistet ein mit Blattgold belegter sitzender Buddha einem neu edierten Exemplar des berühmten Rot-Blauen Stuhls Gesellschaft, den der niederländische Designer Gerrit Rietveld 1917 entworfen hatte. • Dans le séjour, un ancien bouddha assis, doré à la feuille, côtoyait une réédition du célèbre fauteuil « rouge-jaune-bleu » créé en 1917 par le designer néerlandais Gerrit Rietveld.

CASA DE LA TORRE

CASA DE LA TORRE

MUSEO ROBERT BRADY
CUERNAVACA

In February 1990, the doors of number 4, Calle Nezahualcóyotl in Cuernavaca swung open to the public, admitting them to the home of the American artist Robert Brady (1928–1986). Brady, born in Iowa to well-off parents who owned their own transport company, developed a passion for the arts at an early age. After studying at The Art Institute of Chicago and the Barnes Foundation in Philadelphia, he left America and moved to Europe, where he settled in Venice. Here he lived in the palace once occupied by the famous Italian artist Filippo de Pisis. This was conveniently located round the corner from Peggy Guggenheim, who was to become Brady's best friend and mentor. Fascinated by Mexico and the country's abundant art, colours and folklore, Brady moved to Cuernavaca and set up home in the Casa de la Torre in 1961. Over the ensuing decades Brady received royalty, diplomats, artists and the international jet set and transformed the house, once part of a Franciscan convent, into a labyrinth of elegant salons, each decorated with remarkable taste and filled with unique collections.

Im Februar 1990 öffneten sich die Türen des in der Calle Nezahualcóyotl Nr. 4 gelegenen Hauses in Cuernavaca, sodass die neugierige Öffentlichkeit sich ein Bild von der Wohnung des amerikanischen Malers Robert Brady (1928–1986) machen konnte. Brady, Sohn aus einer wohlhabenden Transportunternehmerfamilie, stammte aus Iowa. Er fühlte sich schon früh zur Kunst hingezogen. Nach dem Studium am Art Institute of Chicago und in der Barnes Foundation in Philadelphia verließ er seine Heimat und zog nach Europa, genauer gesagt nach Venedig. Dort lebte er im Palast des berühmten Malers Filippo de Pisis, angenehmerweise ganz in der Nähe von Peggy Guggenheim, die zu seiner besten Freundin und Mentorin wurde. 1961, als ihn die Kunst, die Farben und die Folklore Mexikos faszinierten, bezog er die Casa de la Torre in Cuernavaca, die einst zu einem Franziskanerkloster gehört hatte. In den folgenden Jahrzehnten empfing Brady Diplomaten, Könige, Künstler und den internationalen Jetset. Und er verwandelte das Haus in ein Labyrinth von eleganten Salons, die er mit bemerkenswertem Geschmack dekorierte und in denen er seine Sammlungen unterbrachte.

En février 1990, les portes de la maison sise au 4 de la Calle Nezahualcóyotl à Cuernavaca se sont ouvertes, et les curieux ont pu visiter la demeure du peintre américain Robert Brady (1928–1986). Né dans l'Iowa, au sein d'une famille aisée propriétaire d'une compagnie de transports, Brady fut attiré par les arts dès son plus jeune âge. Après des études à l'Art Institute of Chicago et à la Barnes Foundation de Philadelphie, il quitta son pays pour s'établir en Europe, à Venise plus précisément, dans le palais du célèbre peintre Filippo de Pisis, agréablement proche de Peggy Guggenheim qui devint sa meilleure amie et son inspiratrice. En 1961, attiré par le Mexique, son art, ses couleurs et son folklore, il s'installa à Cuernavaca dans la Casa de la Torre qui faisait jadis partie du couvent franciscain. Durant les décennies qui suivirent, il accueillit des diplomates, des rois, des artistes et des membres de la jet-set, et transforma l'habitation en un dédale de salons élégants, décorés avec un goût remarquable et abritant des collections uniques.

PP. 86–87 Pots of sansevieria are ranged along the stone balustrade of Robert Brady's last home, silent sentries standing guard over the front door. • Auf der Brüstung der Steinbalustrade vorm Haus des verstorbenen Robert Brady reihen sich die eingetopften Sansevierien. • Sur l'appui de la balustrade en pierre de la maison du regretté Robert Brady, des sansevières en pots sont alignées somme des sentinelles muettes.

P. 89 The staircase leading to the kitchen and the dining room. • Die Steintreppe, die zu Küche und Esszimmer führt. • L'escalier qui mène à la cuisine et à la salle à manger.

↑ A pre-Columbian statue strikes a meditative pose in the window. • Die präkolumbianische Statue in der Fensterlaibung scheint in der Sonne zu meditieren. • Une statue précolombienne semble méditer au soleil dans l'embrasure d'une fenêtre.

→ The balcony of Brady's studio looks out onto the ancient convent with its imposing tower and stairways. • Blick von Bradys Atelierbalkon auf den Turm und die Treppe des früheren Klosters. • Du balcon de l'atelier de Brady, on peut admirer la tour et les escaliers de l'ancien couvent.

ROBERT
BRADY
3 February 1928
20 June 1986

PP. 92–93 The walls of this room are decorated with eye-catching masks. The bouquet of flowers was crocheted by Brady's cook. • Dieser Gewölbesaal ist mit außergewöhnlichen Masken dekoriert. Der Blumenstrauß ist eine Häkelarbeit von Bradys Köchin. • Cette salle voûtée est décorée de masques étonnants. Le bouquet de fleurs est un ouvrage au crochet réalisé par la cuisinière de Brady.

↑ Robert Brady welcomed numerous celebrities to his salon in Casa de la Torre, among them Hollywood stars such as Rita Hayworth and Ava Gardner. His famous neighbour, the painter Tamara de Lempicka, had also chosen Cuernavaca as her favorite getaway, and was one of his closest friends. • In seinem Salon in der Casa de la Torre empfing Robert Brady eine beeindruckende Zahl berühmter Gäste, darunter Filmstars aus Hollywood wie Rita Hayworth und Ava Gardner. Auch seine berühmte Nachbarin, die Malerin Tamara de Lempicka, hatte sich für Cuernavaca als liebsten Zufluchtsort entschieden. Sie gehörte zu seinem engsten Freundeskreis. • Dans son salon de la Casa de la Torre, Robert Brady recevait un nombre impressionnant d'hôtes célèbres parmi lesquels figuraient des stars du cinéma hollywoodien comme Rita Hayworth et Ava Gardner. Sa célèbre voisine, la peintre Tamara de Lempicka qui, elle aussi, avait choisi Cuernavaca comme son refuge de prédilection était une de ses amies les plus proches.

→ The kitchen is full of Mexican decorative motifs; note the traditional faience tiles that often decorate kitchens in the region. • In der Küche wimmelt es nur so von typisch mexikanischen, dekorativen Objekten. Besonders auffällig sind die traditionellen Fayence-Kacheln, mit denen die Küchen der Region häufig geschmückt sind. • La cuisine abonde d'éléments décoratifs typiquement mexicains ; on y remarque en particulier la présence des carreaux en faïence traditionnels qui ornent souvent les cuisines dans la région.

PP. 96 and 97 As a painter, Brady was sensitive to the charms of Mexican arts and craft. This bathroom is resplendent with traditional tilework. • Der Maler liebte die mexikanische Volks- und Handwerkskunst. Das Badezimmer ist mit traditionellen Kacheln ausgestattet. • Le peintre était très sensible au folklore et à l'artisanat mexicains. Carreaux traditionnels dans cette salle de bains.

← The interiors of the Casa de la Torre overflow with the heterogeneous objects brought back by the owner from his many voyages around the world or from his previous houses. • Die Innenräume der Casa de la Torre sind geradezu überbordend mit einer Unmenge bunt zusammengewürfelter Objekte ausgestattet, die der Hausherr auf seinen zahlreichen Reisen durch die ganze Welt gesammelt oder von früheren Wohnsitzen mitgebracht hatte. • Les intérieurs de la Casa de la Torre croulent sous une masse d'objets hétéroclites ramenés par le maître de maison de ses multiples voyages autour du monde ou provenant de ses résidences précédentes.

↑ In the bathroom, a gilt Buddha figure occupies a niche with a Moorish arch. • Im Badezimmer steht ein vergoldeter Buddha in einer Nische mit maurischen Bögen. • Dans la salle de bains aux arches mauresques, un bouddha se dresse dans une niche.

↑ Nothing escaped Brady's obsessive decorative attentions: in his bedroom, the doors of the wardrobe are covered with very elaborate openwork patterns. • Nichts war vor der verrückten Dekorationsleidenschaft Bradys sicher. In seinem Schlafzimmer sind selbst die Türen seiner Kleiderschränke von exotischen, fein ausgearbeiteten durchbrochenen Wandungen bedeckt. • Rien n'échappait à la folie de la décoration de Brady et, dans sa chambre à coucher, même les portes de ses garde-robes se couvrent de claustras exotiques, très élaborées.

→ An oversize plaster scallop shell crowns the wardrobe doors. • Über den Türen zu den Kleiderkammern prangt eine überdimensionale Muschelschale aus Gips. • Une coquille en plâtre surdimensionnée surmonte la porte des garde-robes.

PP. 102–103 In this room, one of the upstairs bedrooms, Brady assembled an audacious mix of styles, juxtaposing Venetian Baroque with the splendours of India and the Moorish influences of Marrakesh. A bedroom that doubles as a work of art. • In einem der Zimmer im Obergeschoss hat Brady mutig die unterschiedlichsten Stile zusammengebracht: venezianischer Barock, reich verzierte Objekte aus Indien und maurische Akzente im Marrakesch-Stil. Das Ergebnis kann sich sehen lassen. • Dans une des chambres à l'étage, Brady a marié avec une belle audace les styles les plus divers: baroque vénitien, splendeurs de l'Inde et accents mauresques dans le style de Marrakech. Le résultat est prodigieux.

VICTOR MANUEL
CONTRERAS

VICTOR MANUEL CONTRERAS

CUERNAVACA

Victor Manuel Contreras is known locally as "maestro", a mark of respect accorded to those who have achieved perfection in their chosen art, discipline or profession. Contreras' sculpting skills have earned him many honorary titles and commissions and his work graces numerous public squares and forecourts of official buildings in his homeland. The master's studio and eye-catching home make the perfect showcase for his creations past and present and work of all shapes and sizes is exhibited alongside classical statues and the work of sculptors he admires. With an eye for theatrical effect, Contreras has filled his spacious salons with paintings by Tamara de Lempicka (with whom he enjoyed a long "loving friendship") and the personal mementoes of Prince Yusupov, who considered him as "a son fallen from heaven". This respected artist and talented storyteller honours Cuernavaca with his charismatic presence and enriches "the town of eternal spring" with a magnificent home and artist's studio destined to become a museum one day.

Hier nennen ihn alle „Maestro". Dieser schmeichelhafte Titel zeigt an, dass jemand sein Fach, eine Kunst oder ein Handwerk vollendet beherrscht, und er zeugt vom Respekt, der Victor Manuel Contreras entgegengebracht wird. Seine Meisterschaft in der Bildhauerei hat ihm einige Ehrentitel und mehr als einen Auftrag eingebracht. Auf berühmten Plätzen und vor den Amtsgebäuden seines Landes stehen seine Werke. Das Atelier des Künstlers und die prächtige Wohnung bilden den geeigneten Rahmen für frühere und aktuelle Werke, die er zusammen mit klassischen Statuen oder Arbeiten von geschätzten Bildhauern arrangiert. Dem Theatralischen nicht abgeneigt, schmückt er seine weitläufigen Salons mit Gemälden von Tamara de Lempicka, mit der ihn lange eine „verliebte Freundschaft" verband, sowie mit persönlichen Erinnerungen an den Fürsten Jussupow, der ihn den „vom Himmel gefallenen Sohn" nannte. Der Hausherr, nicht nur ein geachteter Künstler, sondern auch ein talentierter Erzähler, beehrt Cuernavaca mit seiner charismatischen Erscheinung und bereichert „die Stadt des ewigen Frühlings" mit einem Wohnhaus und einem Atelier, die wohl eines Tages zum Museum werden.

Tout le monde l'appelle « maestro », et ce titre ronronnant qui indique la perfection dans une discipline, un art ou un métier, enveloppe Victor Manuel Contreras comme une belle cape de velours noir. Il faut dire que sa maîtrise de la sculpture lui a valu maints titres honorifiques, plus d'une commande et des places d'honneur sur les places et devant les bâtiments officiels de son pays. Dans son atelier comme dans sa superbe habitation, le maître expose ses créations d'hier et d'aujourd'hui en disposant ses œuvres de toutes tailles à côté de statues classiques ou d'œuvres de sculpteurs qu'il admire. Avec un penchant pour l'effet théâtral, il décore ses vastes salons avec des toiles de Tamara de Lempicka à qui le lia longtemps une « amitié amoureuse » et des souvenirs personnels du prince Youssoupov qui le surnomma « le fils tombé du ciel ». Conteur de talent, artiste respecté, le maître des lieux honore Cuernavaca de sa présence charismatique et enrichit « la ville du printemps éternel » d'une demeure et d'un atelier qui seront un jour un musée.

PP. 104–105 In Victor Manuel Contreras' house, the inner courtyard is awash with plant life. An old stone statue of a lion keeps company with an imposing fountain. • Der Innenhof des Hauses von Victor Manuel Contreras ist von wuchernden Pflanzen umgeben. Die alte Steinskulptur eines liegenden Löwen leistet der Fontäne des Brunnens Gesellschaft. • Dans la maison de Victor Manuel Contreras, la cour intérieure se couvre d'une végétation abondante. Une ancienne statue en pierre représentant un lion couché tient compagnie à une imposante fontaine.

P. 107 This 19th-century copy of an antique Roman bronze stands enthroned on a pedestal near the front door. • Auf einem Sockel am Eingang steht die im 19. Jahrhundert angefertigte Replik einer Bronzeskulptur aus der römischen Antike. • Sur un socle, près de l'entrée, la copie 19e d'un bronze de l'Antiquité romaine.

← This antique statue, enshrined in an alcove just off the main staircase, is a fitting testimony to the beauty of Aztec art. • In einer Nische seitlich der großen Treppe zeugt eine uralte Statue von der Schönheit der aztekischen Kunst. • Dans une niche près du grand escalier, une statue très ancienne témoigne de la beauté de l'art aztèque.

↑ A magnificent portrait of a woman by Tamara de Lempicka, who was a close friend of Maestro Contreras, enjoys a place of honour over an old sideboard. The sculptures on the sideboard are by the artist-owner of the house. • Ein wunderbares Frauenporträt, ein Original Tamara de Lempickas, die eine Freundin von Maestro Contreras war, hat einen Ehrenplatz über einer alten Anrichte gefunden. Die Skulpturen, die auf dem Möbelstück stehen, sind Werke des Hausherrn. • Un magnifique portrait de femme de la main de Tamara de Lempicka, amie intime de Maestro Contreras, a trouvé une place d'honneur au-dessus d'un bahut ancien. Les sculptures sur le meuble sont des œuvres du maître de maison.

PP. 110–111 The spacious landing of the main entrance has been transformed into a stage on which the owner of the house has imagined a grandiose décor of sturdy wooden benches, 19th-century bronze lamps, a turn-of-the-century table and the copy of an antique statue straight out of Pompeii. • Der große Treppenabsatz des Haupteingangs wurde gekonnt ausgestattet. Der Hausherr weiß, wie man mit soliden Sitzbänken, Bronzeleuchten aus dem 19. Jahrhundert, einem Tisch der Jahrhundertwende und der Replik einer antiken Statue aus Pompeji die größtmögliche Wirkung erzielt. • Le grand palier de l'entrée principale a été décoré avec un sens inné du spectacle. Le maître de maison sait tirer le maximum des banquettes robustes, de quelques luminaires en bronze 19e siècle, d'une table fin de siècle et de la copie d'une statue antique digne de Pompéi.

↑ Victor Manuel Contreras has also proved to be a master in the art of flower arranging. • Victor Manuel Contreras ist auch ein Meister in der Kunst des Blumenarrangements. • Victor Manuel Contreras est aussi passé maître dans l'art de composer les bouquets.

→ The walls of this little saloon are covered in works from the artist's private collection. • Die Wände des kleinen Salons sind mit Werken geschmückt, die zur Privatsammlung des Künstlers gehören. • Les murs d'un petit salon s'ornent d'œuvres qui font partie de la collection privée de l'artiste.

→ Under the guiding hand of an architect, the owner of this sumptuous residence has infused his home with Hollywood glamour. The impressive collection of artworks and classical furniture, not to mention the monumental fireplace in the main room, make this a home fit for a star. • Mit Hilfe eines Architekten hat der Hausherr eine Wohnwelt im Stil Hollywoods eingerichtet. Die Kunstwerke, das klassische Mobiliar und der prächtige, monumentale Kamin sind dem Domizil eines Filmstars ebenbürtig. • Avec l'aide d'un architecte, le maître de maison a aménagé une demeure dans l'esprit hollywoodien. Les œuvres d'art, le mobilier classique et la superbe cheminée monumentale sont dignes de la propriété d'une star.

A VILLAGE HOUSE

A VILLAGE HOUSE

MORELOS

Secluded behind a thick pink-ochre coloured wall and shielded by a massive front door designed to keep out the most prying of eyes, it's clear that those who retreat here are determined to cut themselves off from the world. No need for a "beware of the dog" sign. If the owners grant you admittance to their inner sanctum, a servant will show you through to a high, light-filled living room where sofas and armchairs are tastefully arranged. Design highlights such as the pale blue-beamed ceiling and beautiful antique furniture reflect the exquisite taste and decorating skills of the masters of the house. Wandering through the cool, calm and spacious interiors, visitors will be impressed by the dining room where the eye is instantly caught by an 18th-century Japanese screen, a solid refectory table and a wooden sculpture of a horse. The bedroom, a masterpiece of sober, understated beauty, houses a magnificent Aztec statue fashioned out of terracotta. But the garden is the real star of the show, its riot of tropical vegetation dotted with vivid splashes of bougainvillea.

Die versteckte Lage hinter einer dicken rötlich ockerfarbenen Mauer und die massive Tür, die vor neugierigen Blicken schützt, verraten schon das Bedürfnis der Bewohner, sich hier für ein Wochenende oder länger aus der Welt zurückzuziehen. Ein Schild nach dem Muster „Bissiger Hund" wird man jedoch vergeblich suchen. Wen die Besitzer willkommen heißen, führt ein Dienstbote in einen hohen, hellen Salon mit makellosen Sofas und Sesseln. Die Decke mit blassblauen Balken und die stilvollen alten Möbel lassen den erlesenen Geschmack und das bemerkenswerte gestalterische Talent der Hausherren erkennen. In diesem weitläufigen und angenehm kühlen Haus beeindruckt das Esszimmer, in dem ein japanischer Wandschirm aus dem 18. Jahrhundert, eine solide Klostertafel und ein geschnitztes Holzpferd die Akzente setzen, oder die schlichte Schönheit eines Schlafraums, in dem eine wunderschöne aztekische Terrakottastatue thront. Der Garten mit seinen Bougainvillea in kräftigen Farben und seiner üppigen Tropenvegetation stellt dabei selbst diese Innenräume in den Schatten.

Le fait qu'elle soit dissimulée derrière un mur épais couleur d'ocre rose et d'une porte massive qui décourage le regard des curieux trahit déjà l'attitude des habitants qui désirent se retirer du monde le temps d'un week-end ou davantage. Ici cependant pas d'écriteau du genre « chien méchant ». Si les propriétaires daignent vous recevoir, le valet vous guidera vers un salon haut et clair dans lequel des canapés et des fauteuils immaculés vous accueilleront. Le plafond à poutres bleu pâle et de très beaux meubles anciens révèlent que les maîtres des lieux ont un goût exquis et un don remarquable pour la décoration. Dans cette vaste maison calme et fraîche, on se laisse facilement séduire par une salle à manger que dominent un paravent japonais 18e, une robuste table de réfectoire et un cheval en bois sculpté. Ou par la sobre beauté d'une chambre à coucher dans laquelle trône une magnifique statue aztèque en terre cuite. Mais le jardin vole la vedette aux espaces intérieurs avec ses bougainvillées aux vives couleurs et sa végétation tropicale exubérante.

PP. 116–117 The pool surrounded by bougainvillea. • Rings um den Swimmingpool blühen Bougainvilleen. • La piscine et ses bougainvillées.

P. 119 This corridor, covered by a protective awning, leads to the bedrooms housed in the outbuildings. • Ein mit einem Wetterdach bedeckter Gang führt zu den Gebäuden, in denen die Schlafzimmer liegen. • Un corridor couvert d'un auvent mène aux bâtiments qui abritent les chambres à coucher.

↑ Access to the different buildings is via an intricate labyrinth of staircases. • Ein wahres Labyrinth von Treppen verbindet die verschiedenen Gebäude. • Un véritable labyrinthe d'escaliers relie les divers bâtiments.

→ The tendrils of an ancient climbing-plant snake upward beside one of the stone columns of the patio. • Die Lianen einer jahrhundertealten Kletterpflanze schlängeln sich neben einer der Steinsäulen des Innenhofs empor. • Les lianes d'une plante grimpante séculaire serpentent autour d'une des colonnes en pierre du patio.

← In this haven of peace, the inhabitants have installed throngs of potted plants around the swimming pool, in perfect harmony with the profuse local vegetation. • Um das Schwimmbecken dieses wahrhaft friedlichen Refugiums haben die Bewohner eine Vielzahl von Topfpflanzen aufgestellt, die mit der üppigen Flora des Ortes perfekt harmonieren. • Autour de la piscine de ce véritable havre de paix, les habitants ont installé un grand nombre de plantes en pot qui s'harmonisent parfaitement avec la végétation abondante du lieu.

PP. 122–123 The garden is a veritable exhibition of exotic plants. They encircle the swimming pool: what could be nicer than to lie in their shade after an invigorating plunge? • In diesem Garten sprießen und gedeihen die exotischen Pflanzen vorzüglich. Das gesamte Schwimmbecken ist von ihnen umgeben, und es tut gut, sich nach ein wohltuenden, erfrischenden Bad in ihrem Schatten auszuruhen. • Le jardin est une véritable explosion de plantes exotiques. Elles encerclent la piscine et il fait bon se reposer dans leur ombre après un délicieux bain revigorant.

PP. 126–127 This tranquil alcove houses a collection of colourful terracotta pots. • Eine Nische beherbergt farbige Terrakottaobjekte. • Une niche abrite des terres cuites polychromes.

PP. 128–129 In the high, luminous salon, the immaculate white walls and armchairs with fitted covers create an agreeably cool atmosphere. • Die hohen, makellos weißen Wände des hellen Wohnzimmers und die mit Schonbezügen abgedeckten Sessel verleihen diesem Raum eine angenehme Frische. • Dans le salon haut et clair, la blancheur immaculée des murs et des fauteuils couverts de housses confère a cette pièce une fraîcheur agréable.

↑ In the monastic bedroom, the only decorative elements are a pre-Colombian terracotta statue and a "Shaker"-style chair. • Die einzigen dekorativen Elemente im geradezu mönchisch wirkenden Schlafzimmer sind eine präkolumbianische Tonskulptur und ein Holzstuhl im „Shaker"-Stil. • Dans la chambre à coucher monacale, les seuls éléments décoratifs sont une statue en terre cuite pré-colombienne et une chaise en bois de style « Shaker ».

→ One of the patios at the bottom of the garden. • Einer der Patios im hinteren Teil des Gartens. • Un des patios au fond du jardin.

ARANGO RESIDENCE

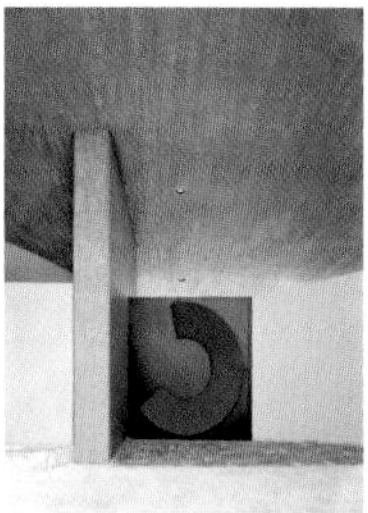

ARANGO RESIDENCE

ACAPULCO

Perched high above Acapulco Bay, architect John Lautner's "Marbrisa" is vertiginous, dramatic and original. For Lautner expert Frank Escher, "what is so beautiful is that it feels like an extension of the topography". The upper level is cantilevered out from the steep slope. Below, boulders thrust inside to become bedroom walls. Completed in 1973, the house was conceived as a weekend retreat. The initial intent was to enclose the upper living deck with glass. The client, however, decided the climate was so mild that it should be left open. Instead, Lautner ringed it with a moat. "He wanted to create the feeling of water flowing into the bay below," recalls Helena Arahuete, who assisted on the project. The free-flowing platform, meanwhile, was devised to block out views of certain buildings. "The concept," she adds, "was to create a feeling of unlimited, open space."

Hoch über der Bucht von Acapulco erhebt sich schwindelerregend, dramatisch und in überwältigender Originalität das Bauwerk „Marbrisa" des Architekten John Lautner. Für den Lautner-Experten Frank Escher ist „das Schöne daran, dass man es als Erweiterung der Landschaft empfindet". Die obere Ebene ist in den steilen Abhang hineingeschnitten. Unterhalb wurde Felsgestein zur Bildung der Schlafzimmerwände in das Innere einbezogen. Das 1973 vollendete Haus war als Feriendomizil geplant. Ursprünglich sollte der obere Wohnbereich verglast werden. Der Auftraggeber beschloss jedoch, ihn angesichts des milden Klimas offen zu lassen. Lautner umgab ihn daraufhin stattdessen mit einem Wasserlauf. „Er wollte den Eindruck von in die Bucht hinabfließendem Wasser hervorrufen", erinnert sich Helena Arahuete, die Lautner bei dem Projekt assistierte. Die frei schwebende Anlage der Plattform sollte den Blick auf bestimmte Gebäude verstellen. „Das Konzept war, ein Gefühl grenzenloser Weite heraufzubeschwören."

Haut perchée au-dessus de la baie d'Acapulco, « Marbrisa », de l'architecte John Lautner, est vertigineuse, spectaculaire et originale. Pour Frank Escher, spécialiste de Lautner, « ce qui est superbe, c'est qu'on dirait une extension de la topographie ». Le niveau supérieur saille de la pente escarpée. Plus bas, des rochers ont été intégrés pour servir de murs aux chambres. Achevée en 1973, la maison fut conçue comme une retraite pour les week-ends. Le niveau supérieur devait être protégé par des baies vitrées mais, compte tenu de la douceur du climat, le propriétaire a décidé de le laisser ouvert aux éléments. Lautner l'a ceint de douves afin, selon Helena Arahuete qui l'a assisté, « de donner une impression d'eau s'écoulant dans la baie en contrebas ». Les formes fluides de la plateforme cachent la vue de certains bâtiments, le concept étant de « créer un espace ouvert et infini ».

PP. 132–133 The curved, sloping concrete roof is anchored into the hill at both ends. The roof is low on the hill side and high on the Bay side, allowing a great view of the sky and the ocean. • Das geschwungene und geneigte Betondach ist auf der Hangseite im Boden verankert, während es auf der Meerseite weit nach oben gezogen ist und so eine einzigartige Sicht auf den Ozean und den Himmel ermöglicht. • Le toit en béton courbe et pentu est ancré dans le sol, bas du côté de la colline et tiré vers le haut du côté de la mer, ce qui permet une vue unique sur l'océan et le ciel.

P. 135 The spectacular house, "Marbrisa," was built in 1973 by the architect John Lautner (1911–1994) for the millionaire Jerónimo Arango; it dominates Acapulco Bay and strikingly resembles a gigantic flying saucer. • „Marbrisa", das spektakuläre, 1973 von John Lautner (1911–1994) für den Milliardär Jeronimo Arango erbaute Anwesen, bietet einen Blick über die Bucht von Acapulco und auf den Pazifischen Ozean. Die Ähnlichkeit des Bauwerks mit einer fliegenden Untertasse ist verblüffend. • La demeure spectaculaire nommée « Marbrisa », construite en 1973 par John Lautner (1911–1994) pour le milliardaire Jerónimo Arango, domine la baie d'Acapulco et l'océan Pacifique. Sa ressemblance avec une gigantesque soucoupe volante est frappante.

→ and PP. 136–137 The upper level is home to an open concrete living terrace, surrounded by a six-foot-wide moat, in which you can swim. The platform is accessed at the entrance by a small bridge. • Die obere Ebene nimmt eine offene Wohnterrasse ein, umgeben von einem 1,80 Meter breiten Wasserlauf, in dem man sogar schwimmen kann. Zu dieser Ebene gelangt man vom Eingang her über eine geschwungene Brücke. • Le niveau supérieur accueille une terrasse en béton servant de séjour ouvert aux éléments. Il est entouré d'une douve de 1,80 m de large dans laquelle on peut nager. On y accède depuis l'entrée par une passerelle aux lignes ondoyantes.

↑ The "flying" staircase is cantilevered from the wall and climbs toward a stretch of green lawn. • Die sich draußen nach oben aufschwingende, „freitragende" Treppe führt zu einer ausgedehnten Grünanlage. • L'escalier « volant » qui se projette hors du mur grimpe vers les hauteurs et s'élance en direction d 'une étendue verte.

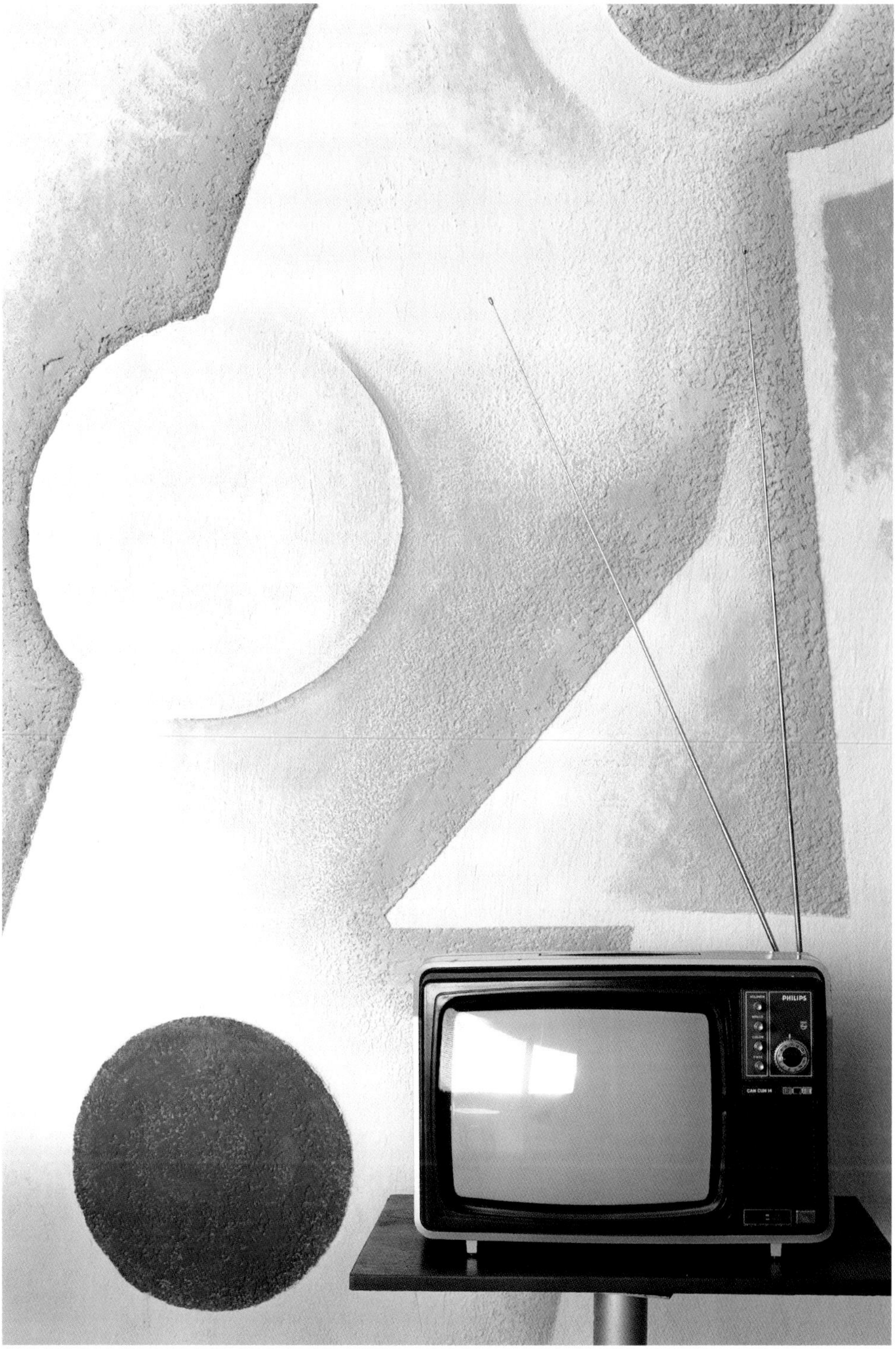
PHILIPS

P. 140 Mexican artist Antonio Farreny created a number of built-in elements for the house. Among them, this geometric metal sideboard. • Der mexikanische Künstler Antonio Farreny schuf für das Haus eine Reihe von Einbau-Elementen, darunter dieses Sideboard aus Metall. • L'artiste mexicain Antonio Farreny a créé plusieurs éléments encastrés pour la maison, dont cette console géométrique en métal.

P. 141 Geometric forms such as these on concrete are a trademark of architect John Lautner's work. • Geometrische Formen, hier auf Beton, sind das Markenzeichen des Architekten John Lautner. • Les formes géométriques, ici sur béton, sont la marque de fabrique de l'architecte John Lautner.

↑ A painting by Jordi Boldó hangs above a copper cabinet created by interior designer Arthur Elrod, for whom Lautner built another famous house, in Palm Springs. • Ein Gemälde von Jordi Boldó hängt über einem Sideboard aus Kupfer nach einem Design von Arthur Elrod. Für den Innenarchitekten und Designer Elrod entwarf Lautner ein nicht weniger berühmtes Haus in Palm Springs. • Une toile de Jordi Boldó au-dessus d'un meuble en cuivre créé par le décorateur Arthur Elrod, pour qui Lautner a construit une autre maison célèbre à Palm Springs.

→ A steel sculpture by Eduardo Wegman mirrors the architecture's curvaceous lines. • Eine Stahlskulptur des Künstlers Eduardo Wegman wiederholt den Kurvenschwung der Architektur. • Une sculpture en acier d'Eduardo Wegman reprend les courbes de l'architecture.

VILLA
TIGRE DEL MAR

VILLA TIGRE DEL MAR

GIAN FRANCO BRIGNONE
COSTA CAREYES

According to Gian Franco Brignone, laying hands on a piece of the Earth is a violation – "so when you violate, do so with care." Before embarking upon his great works, the respectful visionary knelt humbly upon the ground and asked the Earth's permission to cover it with the splendid buildings he saw in his mind's eye. Brignone, known as "the saviour of Careyes", has worked in close collaboration with his brother Marco and the architects Marco Aldaco, Gilbert Trigano, Diego Villaseñor and Jean-Claude Galibert, enriching this unique collection of coves, rocks and beaches with five spectacular villas dedicated to the five senses. The latest in the series, the "Tigre del Mar", is perched on a clifftop, its wild elegance merging with the natural beauty of its surroundings. The Sea Tiger's faded blue façade, sculpted coral-coloured trees, snow-white interiors and beautiful library with a long ladder leant against the façade "to encourage celestial spirits to roam up and down" embodies its creator's respect for nature and love of beauty.

Sich einen Teil der Erde anzueignen, bedeutet für Gian Franco Brignone, ihr Gewalt anzutun, und „wenn man ihr schon Gewalt antut, dann muss man es wenigstens richtig machen". So hat sich der große Visionär von Careyes vor Beginn der Arbeiten demütig hingekniet und die Erde um Erlaubnis gebeten, sie mit seinen Gebäuden zu bedecken. Seither gilt er als „Retter von Careyes". Mit Hilfe seines Bruders Marco und Architekten wie Marco Aldaco, Gilbert Trigano, Diego Villaseñor und Jean-Claude Galibert hat er diese weltweit einzigartige Flucht von Buchten, Stränden und Klippen um fünf spektakuläre Villen bereichert, die den fünf Sinnen gewidmet sind. Die Letzterbaute heißt „Tigre del Mar"; sie erstrahlt auf dem Gipfel einer Klippe in all ihrer wilden Schönheit. Mit einer Fassade in verwaschenem Blau, korallenfarbenen Baumskulpturen, schneeweißen Innenraumakzenten und einer großen Bibliothek, vor der eine lange Leiter „die himmlischen Geister zum Auf- und Absteigen ermuntert", zeugt das Bauwerk vom Erfolgsstreben, der Achtung vor der Natur und der Liebe zur Schönheit seines Schöpfers.

Pour Gian Franco Brignone, s'emparer d'un morceau de la planète est un acte de violence, et « quitte à faire violence, il faut le faire doucement ». Avant d'entamer ses travaux, le grand visionnaire de Careyes s'est agenouillé humblement et a demandé à la terre l'autorisation de la couvrir de bâtiments nés de son imagination. Depuis, il est devenu le « sauveur de Careyes ». Avec l'aide de son frère Marco et des architectes Marco Aldaco, Gilbert Trigano, Diego Villaseñor et Jean-Claude Galibert, il a enrichi cet enchaînement de baies, de plages et de rochers unique au monde de cinq villas spectaculaires dédiées aux cinq sens. La plus récente, le « Tigre del Mar », rugit au sommet d'une falaise et resplendit de toute sa beauté sauvage. Avec sa façade d'un bleu délavé, ses arbres sculptés couleur corail, ses intérieurs blancs comme neige et sa bibliothèque devant laquelle est appuyée une longue échelle « pour encourager les esprits célestes à monter et à descendre », elle incarne la volonté de réussir, le respect de la nature et l'amour de la beauté de son créateur.

PP. 144–145 The giant palapa forms a protective canopy, shielding the house from the sun. This natural shelter is formed of thick creeper-entwined tree trunks, reaching up to support a conical roof covered with dried palm leaves. • Unter der riesigen Palapa ist das Haus vor der Sonne geschützt. Die Baumstämme, um die sich mächtige Lianen ranken, tragen eine kegelförmige Haube, die mit getrockneten Palmzweigen gedeckt ist. • La maison s'abrite du soleil sous la gigantesque palapa. Les troncs d'arbre qu'enlacent de grosses lianes supportent un chapeau conique recouvert de branches de palmier séchées.

P. 147 In this beautiful azure blue bedroom a staircase leads up to a sumptuous bed hidden away on a mezzanine. • In diesem azurblauen Schlafzimmer führt eine Treppe auf eine Plattform, die mit einem großen Bett ausgestattet wurde. • Dans une chambre à coucher bleu azur, un escalier mène à une plateforme garnie d'un grand lit.

PP. 148–149 Beneath a gigantic palapa and an elegant tower a shimmering blue swimming pool stretches away towards the ocean. • Vor einem trutzenden Turm und einer gigantischen Palapa erstreckt sich der Swimmingpool zum Meer hin. • La piscine s'étend vers la mer au pied d'une tour élégante et d'une palapa aux dimensions généreuses.

→ A tropical creeper, artistically entwined around one of the palapa's supporting trunks. • Auf einer Stütze der Palapa rankt sich das Muster einer Liane. • Le beau dessin d'une liane sur un des troncs supportant la palapa.

↑ An eye-catching geometric symbol, engraved on the floor in the entrance hall, and a magnificent terracotta statue pay tribute to the ancient tribes of Mexico. • Ein geometrisches Symbol schmückt den Boden im Eingangsbereich. Die prächtige Terrakottastatue erinnert an die Ureinwohner Mexikos. • Dans l'entrée, le sol est incrusté d'un motif symbolique géométrique. Une superbe statue en terre cuite évoque les anciens habitants du Mexique.

→ Leaning against a cerulean blue wall in the library, this tapering ladder with its worn wooden rungs bleached by the elements is supposed to attract celestial spirits and beings from other worlds. • Gegen die leuchtend blaue Wand der Bibliothek wurde eine riesige, ausgebleichte Leiter gelehnt, die Geister, möglicherweise aber auch Außerirdische, anziehen soll. • Adossée au mur bleu vif de la bibliothèque, une très haute échelle en bois blanchi par les éléments est censée attirer les esprits et (éventuellement) les extra-terrestres.

PP. 154 and 155 With its instant evocation of the sea and the sky, blue is one of Gian Franco Brignone's favourite colours. • Gian Franco Brignone liebt Blau, die Farbe des Himmels und des Meeres. • Gian Franco Brignone adore le bleu, couleur du ciel et de la mer.

↑ The walls of the open-air living room are a vibrant shade of yellow. The African sculptures of water-bearers date from the 1950s. • Knallgelb sind die Wände des Freiluftsalons. Die afrikanischen Wasserträgerinnen stammen aus den 1950er Jahren. • Les murs du salon en plein air sont jaune vif. Les porteuses d'eau africaines datent des années 1950.

→ An original "rest corner" in the open entranceway. • Eine außergewöhnliche Ruhezone im offenen Eingangsbereich. • Dans l'entrée ouverte, un coin repos inhabituel.

PP. 158 and 159 In the entrance hall a banister painted in watery blue trompe-l'œil ascends to the upper floor. The polished stucco steps of the staircase are painted in yellow to harmonise with the walls. Upstairs the staircase takes on the texture and colour of stone. • Aus der Eingangshalle weist ein Trompe-l'œil-Handlauf in den oberen Stock. Die gelben Treppenstufen aus poliertem Gips sind farblich auf die Mauern abgestimmt. Oben passt sich die Treppe der Farbe und Struktur des Steins an. • Dans le hall d'entrée, une rampe d'escalier peinte en trompe-l'œil s'élance vers l'étage supérieur. Les marches en stuc poli s'harmonisent avec les murs. À l'étage, la palette change de nuances et l'escalier imite la couleur et la structure de la pierre.

VILLA SOL DE ORIENTE

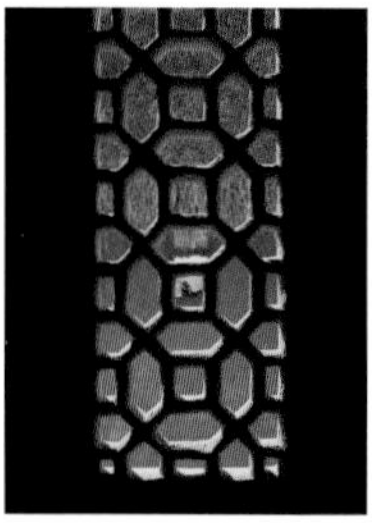

VILLA SOL DE ORIENTE

COSTA CAREYES

Sol de Oriente and Sol de Occidente, the twin houses Gian Franco Brignone built in collaboration with the architect Jean-Claude Galibert, stand on opposite sides of Angel Bay in Careyes. The vividly coloured façades of these superb residences, perched atop the rocks, stand out against the turquoise sky, forming a stunning image on one of Mexico's most beautiful coasts. Sol de Oriente, resplendent in tones of rich red ochre, is managed by Gian Franco's son, Giorgio Brignone, who defends Careyes with the same passion as his father. The colour of this spacious house's façade was inspired by the flamboyant sunsets guests marvel at from the veranda each night, savouring a margarita or a glass of champagne. Sol de Oriente (and Sol de Occidente) can be rented for private use, together with the services of an impeccable and courteous staff who do their utmost to make your stay unforgettable. Sol de Oriente's charms are reserved for those who can afford the extravagant bill that goes with such luxurious surroundings. But, after all, the experience is priceless.

Sol de Oriente und Sol de Occidente, die beiden Häuser, die Gian Franco Brignone in Zusammenarbeit mit dem Architekten Jean-Claude Galibert bauen ließ, liegen zu beiden Seiten der Angel Bay in Careyes einander gegenüber. Hoch auf den Felsengipfeln an einer der schönsten Küsten Mexikos zeichnet sich dieses Zwillingspaar mit seinen leuchtenden Farben vor dem türkisblauen Himmel ab. Verwaltet wird es von Giorgio Brignone, Gian Francos Sohn, der sich ebenso leidenschaftlich wie sein Vater für die Interessen von Careyes einsetzt. Sol de Oriente besticht mit seinen rötlichen Ockertönen, der Farbe des unvergesslichen Sonnenuntergangs, den die Mieter der geräumigen Villa abends bei einem Glas Margarita oder Champagner bewundern können. In Sol de Oriente (wie auch in Sol de Occidente) kann man sich einmieten. Dazu gehört der perfekte Service des höflichen und freundlichen Personals, das alles für einen angenehmen Aufenthalt der wenigen Auserwählten tut, die es sich leisten können, eine sagenhafte Rechnung zu begleichen. Gleichwohl: Sol de Oriente ist ein Traumort – und Träume haben bekanntlich ihren Preis.

Sol de Oriente et Sol de Occidente, les deux maisons que Gian Franco Brignone a fait construire avec la participation de l'architecte Jean-Claude Galibert, se font face de part et d'autre de la Angel Bay à Careyes. Ces magnifiques jumelles aux vives couleurs, perchées au sommet des rochers, se découpent sur le ciel turquoise d'une des plus belles côtes du Mexique. Gérée par Giorgio Brignone, le fils de Gian Franco, qui défend les intérêts de Careyes avec la même passion que son père, Sol de Oriente séduit par ses teintes d'ocre rouge, couleur de l'inoubliable coucher de soleil que les locataires de cette vaste demeure peuvent admirer chaque soir, une verre de Margarita ou de champagne à la main. Il est en effet possible de louer Sol de Oriente (et Sol de Occidente), ainsi que le service inégalé d'un personnel courtois et souriant qui fait tout pour rendre agréable le séjour des quelques élus qui peuvent se permettre le luxe de régler une note mirobolante. Mais qu'importe, Sol de Oriente est un endroit de rêve, et les rêves, comme chacun sait, ont leur prix.

PP. 160–161 The swimming pool offers breathtaking views, looking out across the rocks and appearing to melt into the turquoise waters below. • Der Swimmingpool über den Felsen und dem Meer scheint in den Horizont überzugehen. • La piscine domine les rochers et la mer, dans laquelle elle semble se prolonger jusqu'à l'horizon.

P. 163 A dog shelters from the sun, lounging in the cool shade of the palapa. A stone staircase ascends to the panoramic terrace. • Der kleine Hund bleibt lieber im Schatten der Palapa. Oberhalb der Steintreppe liegt die Panoramaterrasse. • Le petit chien préfère rester à l'ombre de la palapa. En haut de l'escalier en pierre se trouve la terrasse panoramique.

P. 164 The yellow, curved walls of the passageway open out onto the garden and the pool. • Der Durchgang zwischen den geschwungenen gelben Mauern führt in den Garten und zum Swimmingpool. • Le passage entre les murs jaunes incurvés donne sur le jardin et la piscine.

P. 165 The latticed canopy above the benches and tables on the terrace casts geometric patterns on the sunflower yellow walls. • Ein Wetterdach, das Bänke und Tische schützt, zeichnet geometrische Muster auf die sonnenblumengelben Wände der Terrasse. • L'auvent qui abrite des bancs et des tables dessine des motifs géométriques sur les murs jaune tournesol de la terrasse.

↑ The staircase leading to the upper floor and the palapa's conical roof has been colourwashed, diluted red pigment daubed on with a simple sponge technique. • Am Treppenaufgang zum Obergeschoss und zur großen Palapahaube wurde eine Rotpigmentlösung mit einem Schwamm aufgetragen. • La cage de l'escalier qui mène à l'étage supérieur et au grand chapeau de la palapa a été badigeonnée de peinture au pigment rouge diluée et appliquée à l'éponge.

→ The caretaker's dogs wait on the main staircase to greet guests. • Die Hunde des Hausmeisters empfangen Besucher freundlich auf den Stufen der großen Treppe. • Les chiens du gardien accueillent les visiteurs sur les marches du grand escalier.

PP. 168–169 Piles of yellow pillows and green silk cushions strewn across the banquettes contrast with the red-orange walls behind. Mexico comes alive in a vibrant tapestryof colours. • Die Bänke sind mit gelben Sitzpolstern und Kissen aus grüner Seide belegt, die einen Kontrast zu den orangeroten Wänden bilden – Mexiko schillert in vielen Farben. • Sur les banquettes s'amoncellent des coussins jaunes et des coussins de soie verte contrastant avec les murs rouge orangé – le Mexique vibre de couleurs.

← In the romantic rotunda looking out across the sea, the seats espouse the voluptuous curves of the wall. In accordance with local tradition, the floor is encrusted with pebbles. • Die Sitzbänke in der zum Meer gelegenen Rotunde passen sich der Krümmung der Mauern an. In den Boden sind nach lokaler Tradition kleine Kieselsteine eingelassen. • Dans la rotonde qui fait face à la mer, les sièges épousent l'incurvation des murs. Le sol, tradition oblige, est incrusté de petits galets.

↑ Exhibited in an alcove in the dining room, these colourful carved wooden masks have been collected from different regions of Mexico. • In einer Nische des Esszimmers wurden farbige Holzmasken aus allen Regionen Mexikos angeordnet. • Disposés dans une niche de la salle à manger, des masques en bois sculpté polychrome, originaires de toutes les régions du Mexique.

CASI CASA

CASI CASA

BARBARA & MAURIZIO BERGER
COSTA CAREYES

"The first time I saw Careyes it brought tears to my eyes," says Barbara Berger. Such a reaction is understandable, especially when Barbara leads you out onto a huge balcony with sweeping views of the Pacific. This is just one of the design highlights of her spacious apartment in the stunning Casitas de Las Flores complex. The "casitas", built by Gian Franco Brignone in collaboration with architects Alberto Mazzoni and Jean-Claude Galibert, seem to be clinging to the rocks above Playa Rosa. With their brightly painted façades and balconies hung with lush bougainvillea, the "casitas" form a refreshing patchwork of colour. And this palette is in perfect keeping with Barbara's original taste and her passion for bringing different styles together under one roof. Her home, resplendent with the multi-coloured hues of an exotic bird, incorporates an antique door from Rajasthan, embroidered Indian fabrics, traditional Mexican furniture and an array of folk curios, which make Casi Casa a veritable feast for the eyes.

„Als ich Careyes zum ersten Mal sah, sind mir die Tränen gekommen", erzählt Barbara Berger. Man versteht ihre Rührung sofort, vor allem wenn man ihr auf den großen Balkon folgt, der auf den Pazifischen Ozean hinausragt und zur weitläufigen Wohnung im fantastischen Komplex der Casitas de Las Flores gehört. Die von Gian Franco Brignone mit Hilfe der Architekten Alberto Mazzoni und Jean-Claude Galibert erbauten „Casitas" schmiegen sich an den Fels, der die Playa Rosa überragt. Ihre in leuchtenden Farben getünchten Fassaden und die üppigen Bougainvilleen wirken wie ein erfrischendes Patchwork. Die Farbpalette dieser Wohnanlage entsprach ganz Barbaras außergewöhnlichem Geschmack und ihrer Vorliebe für einen Stilmix. In dieser Wohnung, bunt wie ein exotischer Vogel, finden sich eine alte Tür aus Rajasthan, bestickte Tücher aus Indien, traditionelle mexikanische Möbel und eine Fülle folkloristischer Nippsachen, die die Casi Casa zu einer wahren Augenweide machen.

« La première fois que j'ai vu Careyes, j'ai pleuré à chaudes larmes », s'exclame Barbara Berger. On comprend facilement son émotion, surtout quand elle vous entraîne sur ce grand balcon qui surplombe l'océan Pacifique et qui fait partie de son vaste appartement dans le complexe sensationnel de Casitas de Las Flores. Construites par Gian Franco Brignone avec l'aide des architectes Alberto Mazzoni et Jean-Claude Galibert, les « casitas » semblent s'accrocher au rocher qui surplombe la Playa Rosa. Avec leurs façades aux couleurs flamboyantes et leurs balcons dissimulés sous des bougainvillées luxuriantes, elles forment un patchwork d'une fraîcheur incomparable. La palette de l'ensemble convenait parfaitement au goût inhabituel de Barbara et à sa prédilection pour les mariages de styles les plus divers. Dans l'habitation bariolée comme un oiseau exotique, on trouve une ancienne porte du Rajasthan, des tissus brodés indiens, des meubles traditionnels mexicains et une foule de bibelots folkloriques qui font de Casi Casa une véritable fête pour l'œil.

PP. 172–173 Barbara and Maurizio Berger like to enjoy their breakfast on this balcony, looking out over the sea. And who can blame them when the view – and the private beach below – is as heavenly as this? • Barbara und Maurizio Berger frühstücken auf dem zum Meer gelegenen Balkon. Privatstrand und Ausblick sind einfach paradiesisch. • Barbara et Maurizio Berger prennent leur petit-déjeuner sur ce balcon donnant sur la mer. La plage privée et la vue sont tout simplement paradisiaques.

P. 175 The bold colours of the "casitas" reflect Mexico's vibrant palette. • In den Farben der „Casitas" spiegelt sich die schillernde Farbpalette Mexikos. • Les couleurs des « casitas » reflètent parfaitement la palette chatoyante du Mexique.

← This adobe bench invites those back from a morning stroll to rest their weary limbs. • Eine Bank aus Adobe lädt müde Spaziergänger zum Ausruhen ein. • Un banc en adobe invite au repos les promeneurs fatigués.

↑ Flamboyant pots of bougainvillea decorate the staircase, adding strident splashes of colour to the décor. • An einer Treppenwindung fällt der Blick auf eine der zahlreichen Topfbougainvilleen. • Au détour d'un escalier, le regard s'attarde sur l'une des nombreuses bougainvillées en pots.

PP. 178–179 The beauty of the fabrics covering the traditional "chaises longues" on the terrace is further enhanced by the Mexican pink walls. The scallop shells encrusted in the walls make original candle-holders. • Auf der Terrasse unterstreicht das mexikanische Rosa die Stoffe, mit denen die traditionellen Chaiselongues bedeckt sind. In die Wände eingelassene Jakobsmuscheln bilden originelle Kerzenhalter. • Sur la terrasse, le rose mexicain accentue les tissus qui recouvrent les chaises longues traditionnelles. Des coquilles Saint-Jacques incrustées dans le mur sont des porte-bougies originaux.

↑ Near the staircase that leads to the terrace of Casi Casa, a little window takes on the air of a work of contemporary art. • Ein kleines Fenster an der Treppe zur Terrasse der Casi Casa wirkt wie ein zeitgenössisches Kunstwerk. • Près de l'escalier qui monte vers la terrasse de Casi Casa, une petite fenêtre prend l'allure d'une œuvre d'art contemporaine.

→ On the guestrooom balcony, the "Calavera Catrina" looks down upon a cushion from Guatemala. • Auf dem Balkon eines Gästezimmers überragt die dunkle Gestalt einer sogenannten Calavera Catrina ein Kissen aus Guatemala. • Sur le balcon d'une chambre d'amis, la Calavera Catrina domine sombrement un coussin déniché au Guatemala.

← Mexican artisans often choose to depict scenes from daily life in their richly coloured works. • Mexikanische Künstler stellen in ihren farbenprächtigen Werken oft Szenen aus dem Alltag dar. • Les artisans mexicains aiment représenter les scènes de la vie quotidienne dans des œuvres aux riches couleurs.

↑ The bold rainbow hues of the fabrics on the terrace make an arresting sight. A sumptuous banquette stands beneath a window from Rajasthan. • Auf der Terrasse begeistern die bunten Stoffe. Hinter einer riesigen Liege beeindruckt das Fenster aus Rajasthan. • Sur la terrasse, les tissus bigarrés enchantent le visiteur. Une fenêtre du Rajasthan domine une immense banquette.

PP. 184–185 A semi-circular alcove, painted in vivid eye-catching pink, stands above the bed in one of the guest rooms. • Eine leuchtend rosa ausgemalte halbkreisförmige Nische krönt das Bett in einem Gästezimmer. • Une niche semi-circulaire, peinte en rose vif, couronne le lit d'une chambre d'amis.

PP. 186 and 187 The Bergers have gone for a creative colour scheme. The painted terracotta mermaid is one of the highlights of the couple's collection of statuettes made by local Mexican craftsmen. • Die Bergers lieben Farben. Die Sirenenfigur aus Terrakotta gehört zur Sammlung von Statuetten mexikanischer Kunsthandwerker. • Les Berger n'ont pas froid aux yeux quand il s'agit de choisir des couleurs. La sirène en terre cuite peinte fait partie d'une collection de statuettes réalisées par des artisans mexicains.

MI OJO

MI OJO

COSTA CAREYES

In 1968, the Italian banker Gian Franco Brignone flew over the west coast of Mexico and discovered Careyes (named after the Carey tortoises that come to lay their eggs in the region). It was love at first exceptional sight. Describing the spectacular beauty of Careyes is a near impossible task; words are unable to convey the magic of these tranquil turquoise waters, majestic rocks and enchanting natural vistas. Seduced by the charms of Careyes, Brignone started out building a modest-sized residence at Careyitos Bay. Then, after constructing a "palapa" house at Playa Rosa and the famous horse-shoe-shaped hotel, El Careyes, he began work on Mi Ojo (My Eye). This stunning house, set opposite an islet, was inspired by the loss of Brignone's right eye. And it makes an unforgettable sight, the contrast between the blinding white and electric blue of its façade, the terrace overlooked by a round-eyed window and the flamboyant sunsets remains engraved upon the memories of all those lucky enough to have gained admittance to the magical "theatre of Careyes".

1968 war der italienische Bankier Gian Franco Brignone mit dem Flugzeug über der mexikanischen Westküste unterwegs, sah die Gegend von Careyes, so genannt wegen der Carey-Schildkröten, die dort ihre Eier ablegen, und verliebte sich in diese außergewöhnliche Landschaft. Die Schönheit von Careyes beschreiben zu wollen, ist verfänglich: Allzu leicht verfällt man dem Zauber türkisblauen Wassers, majestätischer Felsen und eines berückenden Panaromablicks. Schon bald darauf ließ Brignone ein erstes bescheidenes Haus in Careyitos Bay errichten, darauf eine Palapa in Playa Rosa und anschließend das berühmte hufeisenförmige Hotel El Careyes. Der Verlust seines rechten Auges regte ihn zum Bau von Mi Ojo (Mein Auge) an, einem spektakulären Wohnhaus mit Blick auf eine kleine Insel. Dieses Haus lädt wirklich zu lyrischen Höhenflügen ein. Die Kontraste zwischen dem blendenden Weiß und dem leuchtenden Hellblau der Fassade, zwischen der Terrasse, wo ein Fenster in Form eines weit geöffneten Auges den Akzent setzt, und dem flammenden Sonnenuntergang hinterlassen einen bleibenden Eindruck bei allen, die einmal im Bannkreis des „Theaters von Careyes" gestanden haben.

En 1968, le banquier italien Gian Franco Brignone survolait la côte ouest du Mexique et la région de Careyes, ainsi nommée à cause des carets qui viennent y déposer leurs œufs, et il tomba amoureux de ce site exceptionnel. Décrire la beauté de Careyes est un exercice périlleux ; on se laisse facilement emporter par la magie des eaux turquoise, les rochers majestueux et le panorama enchanté. Brignone n'a pas tardé à faire construire une première demeure modeste à Careyitos Bay. Puis, après avoir bâti une maison palapa à Playa Rosa et le célèbre hôtel El Careyes en forme de fer à cheval, il a entamé la construction de Mi Ojo, Mon Œil, une maison spectaculaire en face d'un îlot, que lui a inspiré la perte de son œil droit. La demeure, elle aussi, invite aux envolées lyriques. Le contraste entre le blanc aveuglant et le bleu électrique de la façade, entre une terrasse dominée par une fenêtre qui imite un œil écarquillé et le coucher de soleil enflammé, restent gravés dans la mémoire de tous ceux qui sont admis dans le cercle magique du « théâtre de Careyes ».

PP. 188–189 and 191 The palm branch roof of the palapa is reflected in the angular pool. • Im Schwimmbecken spiegelt sich die riesige Haube der Palapa. • La piscine anguleuse reflète l'énorme chapeau de la palapa.

↑ → Blue is one of Gian Franco Brignone's favourite colours. • Gian Franco Brignone liebt die Farbe Blau. • Gian Franco Brignone adore la couleur bleue.

PP. 194–195 The architecture of Mi Ojo is full of symbolism. The round window and the interlacing circles that form part of the stunning wall fresco were inspired by the loss of Brignone's right eye. • Die Architektur von Mi Ojo ist symbolträchtig. Das Rundfenster und die Kreise des Wandfreskos erinnern an Brignones Verlust seines rechten Auges. • L'architecture de Mi Ojo est riche en symboles. La fenêtre ronde et les cercles entrelacés d'une fresque sur le mur évoquent la perte subie par le maître des lieux.

↑ In a corner of the roof terrace of villa Mi Ojo, a stone table and the sculpture that crowns it are like strange, petrified plant forms. The walls with their bright blue wash harmonize with the colours of sea and sky. • Der steinerne Tisch und die auf ihrem Sockel thronende Skulptur in einem Winkel der Terrasse der Villa Mi Ojo ähneln seltsamen, versteinerten pflanzlichen Formen. Die mit einem lebhaften Blau getünchten Wände harmonieren mit der intensiven Farbe von Himmel und Meer. • Dans un recoin de la terrasse au sommet de la villa Mi Ojo, la table en pierre et la sculpture qui trône sur sa tablette ressemblent à d'étranges formes végétales pétrifiées. Les murs badigeonnés d'un bleu vif s'harmonisent avec la couleur du ciel et de la mer.

→ On the broad terrace of Gian Franco Brignone's house, a pergola made of a lattice of dead branches protects the sun-lover, filtering out the fiercest rays. • Eine mit einer Lattenkonstruktion aus Astwerk erbaute Pergola auf der großen Terrasse des Hauses von Gian Franco Brignone schützt die Sonnenanbeter und filtert allzu aggressive Strahlen. • Sur la grande terrasse de la maison de Gian Franco Brignone, une pergola construite avec un lattis de branches mortes protège les amateurs de soleil et filtrent les rayons trop agressifs.

↑ The bedroom, with its all-white décor, exudes an atmosphere of perfect calm. • Das ganz in Weiß gehaltene Schlafzimmer verbreitet eine fast unwirkliche Stimmung. • Ambiance irréelle dans la chambre maîtresse, tout habillée de blanc.

→ A circular window – the famous "eye" – in one of the guest rooms, glimpsed from the panoramic terrace. • In einem Gästezimmer blickt man durch das Rundfenster – das berühmte „Auge" – auf die Panoramaterrasse. • Au niveau de la terrasse panoramique, une fenêtre circulaire – le fameux « œil » – dans une chambre d'hôtes.

CASA
DOS ESTRELLAS

CASA DOS ESTRELLAS

LUCIANA PALUZZI & MICHAEL SOLOMON
COSTA CAREYES

Leaving Manzanillo airport and driving up the coast road towards Puerto Vallarta, the view opens out into vistas of lush vegetation. Groves of coconut palms and banana trees stand out against the azure waters of the Pacific, marking the edge of a mysterious jungle crawling with snakes, scorpions, tarantulas and crocodiles. These exotic surroundings appear to be straight out of a James Bond film. And when you first sight the fortress-like Casa dos Estrellas with its Hollywood-style pool and gigantic palapa, it's easy to believe that you're living the fictional lifestyle of 007. Luciana Paluzzi and Michael Solomon originally came to Careyes on holiday but, seduced by the breathtaking ocean views, they ended up building a spectacular house here complete with clifftop balcony (designed by the renowned architect Manolo Mestre). The mistress of Casa dos Estrellas (the House of Two Stars) is an actress who starred in the James Bond film "Thunderball". Luciana and Michael can certainly pride themselves on owning a sensational home in one of the world's most extraordinary settings.

Wenn man den Flughafen in Manzanillo hinter sich gelassen hat und die Küstenstraße nach Puerto Vallarta entlangfährt, zeigt sich eine beeindruckende Pflanzenwelt: Unzählige Kokospalmen und Bananenstauden trennen die azurblauen Gewässer des Pazifischen Ozeans vom geheimnisvollen Dschungel, in dem Schlangen, Skorpione, Taranteln und Krokodile leben. Der perfekte Schauplatz für einen James-Bond-Film. Bei der Ankunft in der festungsartigen Casa dos Estrellas mit dem Schwimmbad im Hollywoodstil und der riesigen Palapa glaubt man sich tatsächlich in die fiktive Existenz von 007 versetzt. Als Luciana und Michael sich für Careyes als Feriendomizil entschieden hatten, bauten sie sich ein einzigartiges Haus. Der Balkon zum Meer, nach Plänen des berühmten Architekten Manolo Mestre, schmiegt sich an einen Felsen, der eine atemberaubende Landschaft überragt. Da überrascht es nicht mehr, dass die Herrin des „Hauses der zwei Sterne" von Beruf Schauspielerin ist und mit dem James-Bond-Film „Feuerball" Teil der Kinolegende wurde. Jedenfalls können Luciana Paluzzi und Michael Solomon stolz darauf sein, ein aufsehenerregendes Domizil an einem der außergewöhnlichsten Orte der Welt zu besitzen.

Après avoir quitté l'aéroport de Manzanillo et longeant la côte qui monte vers Puerto Vallarta, on est agréablement surpris par la végétation et par les innombrables cocotiers et bananiers qui séparent le Pacifique aux eaux d'azur de la jungle mystérieuse peuplée de serpents, de scorpions, de tarentules et de crocodiles. Un cadre digne d'un film de James Bond. En s'approchant de la Casa dos Estrellas avec son allure de forteresse, sa piscine hollywoodienne et sa palapa démesurée, on est persuadé d'avoir été projeté dans l'existence fictive de 007. Ayant choisi Careyes pour y passer ses vacances, Luciana et Michael se sont construit une demeure sans pareille. Ce balcon sur la mer, bâti d'après les plans du célèbre architecte Manolo Mestre, est perché au sommet d'un rocher qui domine un paysage à couper le souffle. On constatera sans surprise que la maîtresse de la « maison des deux étoiles », actrice de cinéma elle-même, est entrée dans la légende avec « Opération Tonnerre », un film de James Bond. En tout cas, Luciana Paluzzi et Michael Solomon peuvent s'enorgueillir de posséder une demeure sensationnelle dans un des lieux les plus extraordinaires qui soient.

PP. 200–201 Perched on the clifftops like an eagle's nest, the Solomons' spectacular home cuts an impressive fortress-like silhouette. • Adlerhorst, beeindruckende Festung – solche Assoziationen passen zu dem spektakulären Haus der Solomons. • Nid d'aigle, forteresse impressionnante – ces termes correspondent parfaitement à la maison des Solomon.

P. 203 This breathtaking view from one of the terraces is typical of the stunning vistas in Careyes. • Der Ausblick von einer der Terrassen ist atemberaubend – wie alle Ausblicke in Careyes. • Depuis l'une des terrasses, la vue est époustouflante. Mais toutes les vues le sont à Careyes.

← In the bedroom of the Casa Dos Estrellas, a shady balcony projects out over the void like a ship's bowsprit, affording the inhabitants a spectacular view over the ocean. • Wie die Galionsfigur eines Schiffes ragt ein schattiger Balkon des Schlafzimmers der Casa dos Estrellas ins Offene und bietet den Bewohnern einen spektakulären Blick aufs Meer. • Dans la chambre à coucher de la Casa dos Estrelos, un balcon ombragé s'élance vers le vide comme la figure de proue d'un bateau et offre à ses habitants une vue spectaculaire sur la mer.

↑ A picturesque path winds down to the private beach. • Eine Treppe windet sich hinunter zum Privatstrand. • Un escalier sinueux descend vers la petite plage privée.

↑ Beneath the shady palm roof of the palapa, a spiral staircase leads to a tower-top terrace. • Unter der Palapa führt eine Wendeltreppe auf die Terrasse, die den oberen Abschluss eines Turmes bildet. Eine zeitgenössische Skulptur spiegelt die kräftigen Farben der Bänke und Mauern. • Sous la palapa, un escalier en colimaçon rejoint la terrasse située au sommet d'une des tours. Une sculpture contemporaine fait écho aux couleurs vives de la banquette et des murs.

→ Bright yellow walls enliven the sunny interior. As you mount the stairs, don't forget to pay your respects to the fish-tailed mermaid on the bas-relief. • Die gelben Wände lassen dieses sonnendurchflutete Interieur erstrahlen. Die Treppe führt an einem Basrelief vorbei, das eine Sirene darstellt. • Les murs jaunes contribuent à égayer cet intérieur ensoleillé. L'escalier passe devant un bas-relief représentant une sirène.

PLAYA ROSA – CASITAS DE LAS FLORES

PLAYA ROSA – CASITAS DE LAS FLORES

COSTA CAREYES

Can there be anyone who has not fantasised about enjoying their own private corner of paradise somewhere at the ends of the earth? Who has not dreamt of lounging in a secluded, thatch-roofed cabana, surrounded by swaying coconut palms, staring out at a distant horizon where the turquoise ocean merges with an almost unbearably blue sky? Welcome to the world of "dolce far niente", where life is lived with the ocean at your feet and your head in the clouds. Relax in an armchair at the clubhouse, fronting the blissful blue of the Pacific, with a long, cool cocktail or dine in the gaily coloured restaurant a stone's throw from your door. The lucky inhabitants of the Casitas de Las Flores have access to a private beach – the small but perfectly formed Playa Rosa – via a staircase or a tiny funicular which rocks along at a snail's pace. Down on Playa Rosa, a vibrant pink restaurant, built like a traditional Mayan house, serves delicious regional specialities and freshly caught fish. Is this just a splendid fantasy? An enticing mirage? Why no, not at all – Costa Careyes is the land where the wildest dreams come true.

Wer hat nicht schon einmal von einem kleinen Privatparadies am anderen Ende der Welt geträumt, dort, wo Meeres- und Himmelsblau miteinander verschmelzen? Vielleicht in einem von Kokospalmen umgebenen Häuschen mit Strohdach, worin man einen glücklichen Alltag genießen könnte? Wer hat nicht schon dem Wunsch nachgehangen, mit den Füßen im Meer und dem Kopf in den Wolken zu leben und dabei auch noch bequem im Sessel zu sitzen? „Dolce far niente" eben, ein Leben nach Lust und Laune. Mit Blick auf den Pazifischen Ozean, Clubhaus und Longdrink in Reichweite und einem kleinen Restaurant in fröhlichen Farben quasi vor der Haustür. In Costa Careyes scheinen die tollsten Fantasien und die geheimsten Wünsche mit Leichtigkeit in Erfüllung zu gehen. Die Glücklichen, die in den Casitas de Las Flores wohnen, brauchen nur ein paar Stufen hinabzusteigen oder die kleine, langsame Seilbahn zu nehmen, um zu dem überschaubaren Strand Playa Rosa zu gelangen, wo ein Restaurant wie ein historischer Maya-Bau sie mit köstlichen Gerichten und fangfrischem Fisch empfängt. Ein Traum? Eine Fata Morgana? Ganz und gar nicht. In Costa Careyes werden Träume wahr.

Qui de nous n'a pas rêvé d'un coin de paradis privé, quelque part, à l'autre bout du monde, là où la mer et le ciel (d'un bleu si intense qu'il en devient presque insoutenable) se confondent et où une petite cabane à toit de chaume, entourée de cocotiers, abriterait un bonheur quotidien sorti tout droit d'un roman à l'eau de rose, genre Barbara Cartland ? Qui de nous n'a pas caressé le désir de vivre sa vie avec la mer à ses pieds, la tête dans les nuages et confortablement blotti dans un fauteuil ? Le « dolce far niente » quoi ! La douceur de vivre absolue. Avec vue sur l'océan Pacifique, club-house, long drink à portée de la main, et un petit restaurant peint en couleurs gaies à deux pas de la porte. À Costa Careyes, les fantasmes les plus fous et les désirs les plus secrets semblent se matérialiser avec une aisance alarmante. Les heureux qui habitent les Casitas de Las Flores n'ont qu'à descendre quelques marches ou prendre un petit funiculaire lent comme un escargot pour aboutir jusqu'à la plage, modeste de dimensions, nommée Playa Rosa et où un restaurant qui ressemble à une vieille demeure maya, agréablement peint en rose, les accueille avec des plats succulents et le poisson le plus frais du monde. Un rêve ? Un mirage ? Pas du tout. Car à Costa Careyes le rêve devient toujours réalité.

PP. 208–209 and 211 Inspired by the décor of traditional Mayan houses, the pink facades of the "casitas" at Playa Rosa have a contemporary feel. • Die Häuser der Playa Rosa sind zwar von den alten Maya-Bauten inspiriert, wirken aber durch den rosafarbenen Anstrich moderner. • Inspirés par les anciennes maison mayas, les bâtiments de la Playa Rosa sont peints en rose, ce qui leur donne un aspect plus contemporain.

PP. 212–213 Coconut palms wave in the breeze on the private beach at Playa Rosa. • Unter den Kokospalmen des Privatstrands von Playa Rosa lässt es sich leben. • Il fait bon vivre sous les cocotiers de la plage privée de Playa Rosa.

← The pink bar is decorated with natural materials such as tree trunks, pebbles, whalebone and an oversized palapa roof. • Die Bar im schönsten Rosa wurde auf sehr schlichte Weise mit natürlichen Materialien eingerichtet: Baumstämme, Kiesel, Palapa und ein stattlicher Walknochen. • Le bar, rose à souhait, a été sobrement décoré avec des matériaux naturels : troncs d'arbre, galets, palapa et un os de baleine.

↑ On the outside, the clubhouse buildings of the Playa Rosa imitate the single-storey Mayan houses and, like them, are roofed with traditional palm-branch thatching. • Das Äußere der Gebäude des Clubhauses der Playa Rosa ist den niedrigen Häusern der Maya nachempfunden: Auch diese Dächer sind auf traditionelle Art und Weise mit Palmzweigen gedeckt. • De l'extérieur, les bâtiments du club-house de la Playa Rosa imitent les maisons basses des Mayas et ils se couvrent également du traditionnel toit en branches de palmier.

↑ Next to a chair covered in eye-catching Mexican pink fabric, a painting of a mermaid is juxtaposed with an antique plaster figure. • In der Nähe eines Sessels in mexikanischem Rosa sind ein Gemälde mit Sirene und eine Gipsbüste antiker Prägung gruppiert. • Près d'un siège habillé de rose mexicain, un tableau représentant une sirène et un plâtre à l'antique se côtoient.

→ The restaurant's rustic décor is enhanced by a palm-leaf palapa roof and bull's-eye windows outlined in vivid pink. • Rosa eingefasste Bullaugen und ein Palapadach unterstreichen den rustikalen Charakter des Restaurants. • Des œils-de-bœuf cerclés de rose vif et un toit en palapa accentuent le caractère rustique du restaurant.

VERANA

VERANA

YELAPA

When a stylist and a film set designer develop a new hotel, there's a good chance the results will be pretty special. In fact, in the case of the Verana, opened by Heinz Legler and Véronique Lièvre in the year 2000, even the journey there is spectacular: this hotel up above the Bay of Banderas can be reached only by boat, then it's a short mule ride up from the boat jetty to this outpost of paradise. Architecture and nature combine here beautifully. All the houses have private gardens, and their interiors, which are furnished with vintage pieces and George Nelson lamps, echo the colours of their surroundings. From guest accommodation to spa and poolside restaurant, everything at this jungle retreat is arranged to perfection—it could well be the finest scene Véronique has ever designed.

Wenn sich eine Stylistin und ein Filmset-Designer zusammen ein Hotel ausdenken, darf man sicher sein, dass es richtig was hermacht. Beim Verana, das Heinz Legler und Véronique Lièvre Ende 2000 eröffneten, ist schon die Anfahrt spektakulär - die Hotelanlage im Dschungel über der Bucht von Banderas ist nur per Boot zu erreichen. Vom Anleger geht es mit Gepäckmaultieren das letzte Stück bergauf, dann hat man einen Außenposten des Paradieses erreicht. Natur und Architektur harmonieren hier wahrlich filmreif. Jedes der kleinen Häuser hat einen privaten Garten; innen wiederholen sich die Farben der Umgebung, dazu kommen Vintage-Möbel und Leuchten von George Nelson. Keine Frage, hier sitzt jedes Stück am richtigen Platz. Das gilt auch für das Spa und das Restaurant am Pool - zusammen mit der eindrucksvollen Natur ist das bestimmt die beste Kulisse, die Véronique je gestaltet hat.

Quand une styliste et un décorateur de cinéma s'associent pour créer un hôtel, on peut s'attendre à du grand art. L'accès au Verana, ouvert par Véronique Lièvre et Heinz Legler en 2000, est déjà spectaculaire en soi. Situé dans la jungle surplombant la baie de Banderas, cet hôtel n'est accessible que par bateau. Et du débarcadère, on gravit avec des mulets de bât les derniers mètres qui mènent à cette antichambre du paradis. Ici, la nature et l'architecture s'harmonisent comme dans un décor de cinéma. Chaque maisonnette a son jardin privé. Orné de meubles vintage et de luminaires de George Nelson, l'intérieur reflète les couleurs de l'environnement. Tout est ici parfaitement à sa place, ce qui vaut aussi pour le spa et le restaurant au bord de la piscine. Implanté dans une nature impressionnante, cet hôtel est certainement le plus beau décor jamais réalisé par Véronique.

PP. 218–219 From the terrace of Verana, the view over the superlative Bay of Banderas is breathtaking; a stay in this exceptional location makes the trip well worthwhile. Arriving by boat and following the mules and their load of luggage up the cliff to reach this paradisiacal location is an unforgettable experience. • Der Blick über die herrliche Bucht von Banderas, der sich von der Terrasse des Verana bietet, ist sagenhaft. Ein Aufenthalt an diesem außergewöhnlichen Ort ist eine Reise wert. Das Verana mit dem Boot anzusteuern und dann den mit dem Gepäck beladenen Maultieren zu Fuß zu folgen, um diesen paradiesischen Winkel zu erreichen, ist ein unvergessliches Erlebnis. • De la terrasse de Verana, la vue sur la magnifique baie de Banderas est à couper le souffle et un séjour dans cet endroit exceptionnel vaut bien l'effort du voyage. Atteindre Verana en bateau et suivre à pied les mulets de bât chargé de bagages pour atteindre ce coin de paradis est une expérience inoubliable.

P. 221 The gardens beside the maisonettes provide guests with the luxury of a calm, shady corner where they can choose their own form of relaxation or enjoy the beauty of the sunset. • Die an die Maisonette-Unterkünfte angrenzenden Gärten bieten den Gästen den Luxus eines privaten ruhigen und schattigen Winkels, wo sie sich nach Gutdünken ausruhen oder den schönen Sonnenuntergang genießen können. • Les jardins attenants aux maisonnettes offrent aux hôtes le luxe d'un coin privé calme et ombragé où ils peuvent se reposer à leur guise ou profiter d'un beau coucher de soleil.

PP. 222–223 In Mexico, sun and sea are one and the same thing; the infinity pool at Verana, merging with the intense blue of the sea, likewise reflects the sky. • In Mexiko sind Himmel und Meer eins. Das Schwimmbad des Verana, das mit dem intensiven Blau des Meeres verschmilzt, macht da keine Ausnahme. • Au Mexique, le ciel et la mer ne font qu'un. À Verana, la piscine se confond aussi bien avec le bleu de la mer qu'elle reflète le bleu du ciel.

← Down a few steps, there is a little private terrace where it is pleasant to relax for a while or enjoy a peaceful breakfast. • Nur wenige Stufen hinab, und es eröffnet sich eine kleine, charmante private Terrasse. Hier kann man sich gut ein Weilchen ausruhen oder in Ruhe frühstücken. • En descendant à peine quelques marches, on découvre une petite terrasse privée pleine de charme où il fait bon se reposer un moment ou prendre son petit déjeuner en toute tranquillité.

PP. 226–227 In this marvelous place, a tribute to the talents of its owners, Heinz Legler and Véronique Lièvre, the terraces and gardens create a delightfully harmonious ensemble. • Die Terrassen und Gärten dieses sehr außergewöhnlichen, von den talentierten Besitzern Heinz Legler und Véronique Lièvre gestalteten Anwesens bilden ein Ensemble perfekter Harmonie. • Dans ce lieu hors du commun imaginé et crée par les maîtres de maison Heinz Legler et Véronique Lièvre, les terrasses et les jardins forment un ensemble d'une harmonie parfaite.

← Inspired by the architectural style of the Bauhaus, the great glazed bays with their pivoted openings afford a superb view over the bay and the sea. The canopy of a palm acts as a brise-soleil and offers the shade and coolness of its leaves. • Die großen, vom Architekturstil des Bauhauses inspirierten Fensterpartien mit ihren rechteckigen, einzeln schwenkbaren Klappen bieten einen beeindruckenden Ausblick auf die Bucht und das Meer. Die Wipfel einer Palme gewähren, wie ein Sonnenschirm, Schatten und Kühle. • Inspirés par l'idiome architectural du Bauhaus, les grandes baies vitrées avec leurs carreaux individuels pivotants offrent une vue impressionnante sur la baie et la mer. Le sommet d'un palmier fait office d'écran et apporte ombre et fraicheur.

PP. 230–231 Comfortable leather-covered tubular-steel chairs reflect a taste for the austere designs of the 1930s. Beyond the glass wall, a veritable jungle of trees and exotic plants brings shade and protects the guests from the sun. • Bequeme, mit Leder bezogene Stahlrohrsessel zeugen von einer Vorliebe für das Design der 1930er Jahre. Hinter den Scheiben spendet ein wahrer Dschungel von Bäumen und exotischen Pflanzen Schatten und schützt die Gäste vor der Sonne. • Des fauteuils confortables en métal tubulaire recouverts de cuir reflètent un certain penchant pour le design épuré des années 1930. Au-delà de la verrière, une jungle d'arbres et de plantes exotiques se charge d'apporter de l'ombre et de protéger les hôtes du soleil.

← ↑ Walls in subtle colours with an antique patina form a perfect background for an exotic mask. Beds with mosquito nets disappear under piles of cushions. • Die zarten und patinierten Farbtöne der Wände sind ein perfekter Hintergrund für die exotische Maske. Die mit Moskitonetzen ausgestatteten Betten verschwinden fast unter einem Berg von Kissen. • Des murs aux tons subtils et patinés à l'ancienne forment le décor parfait pour un masque exotique. Des lits équipés de moustiquaire disparaissent sous un amoncèlement de coussins.

VERANA DAY SPA

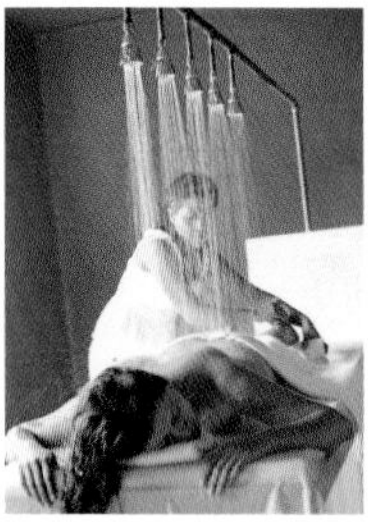

VERANA DAY SPA

AT VERANA,
JALISCO

Following on from their successful Jungle Spa, which is for Hotel Verana guests only, Véronique Lièvre and Heinz Legler decided to add an idyllic day spa for up to 16 visitors per day. Opened in late 2008, it offers a relaxing body-temperature Watsu pool and treatments featuring extracts of papaya, avocado or coconut sourced from the nearby jungle.

Nach dem Erfolg des Jungle Spa – exklusiv für Gäste ihres Hotels Verana – haben Véronique Lièvre und Heinz Legler Ende 2008 dieses idyllische Day Spa für Tagesgäste eröffnet. Maximal 16 Besucher pro Tag entspannen hier im Watsu-Pool mit körperwarmem Wasser sowie bei Pflegeritualen mit Extrakten aus Papayas, Avocados oder Kokosnüssen, die im nahen Dschungel wachsen.

Voyant le succès du Jungle Spa – proposé exclusivement aux hôtes de leur hotel Verana –, Véronique Lièvre et Heinz Legler ont ouvert fin 2008 ce Day Spa idyllique. L'entrée est limitée à 16 visiteurs par jour : ils se relaxent ici dans un bassin watsu rempli d'eau à température du corps ou savourent les rituels de soins à base d'extraits de papaye, d'avocat et de noix de coco, qui poussent dans la jungle toute proche.

PP. 234–235 The walls of the cubic treatment-building have been brushed with a dilute blue wash. From this eagle's nest, there is an impressive view over the Bay of Banderas. A few steps down, protected from the sun and wind, the Watsu pool, whose temperature mirrors that of the human body. • Die Mauern dieses würfelförmigen Gebäudes, in dem sich Räumlichkeiten zur Körperpflege befinden, wurden mit einer Lavur verwaschenen Blaus gestrichen. Von diesem unvergleichlichen, hochgelegenen Ausguck bietet sich ein beeindruckender Blick auf die Bucht von Banderas. Nur ein paar Stufen tiefer liegt, vor Sonne und Wind geschützt, das Watsu-Becken, dessen Wasser auf die Temperatur des menschlichen Körpers gebracht wurde. • Les murs du bâtiment cubique qui renferme l'espace pour les soins ont été badigeonnés avec un lavis bleu délavé et, de ce nid d'aigle sans pareil, on a une vue impressionnante sur la baie de Banderas. À peine quelques marches plus bas, protégé du soleil et du vent, on découvre le bassin Watsu dont l'eau a été adaptée à la température du corps humain.

P. 237 This place is very clearly beside the sea. Who could have guessed that it is also a few steps from the jungle? • Wohlwissend, dass dieser Ort so nah am Meer liegt, kann man sich kaum vorstellen, dass auch der Dschungel nur ein paar Schritte entfernt ist. • Sachant que ce lieu se trouve si proche de la mer, il est impossible de deviner qu'il se trouve aussi à deux pas de la jungle.

PP. 238–239 Heinz Legler and Véronique Lièvre have again drawn from their profound knowledge of styles to create a spa whose outline is directly inspired by the interwar architectural style and houses designed by Le Corbusier. • Heinz Legler und Véronique Lièvre haben auch hier ihre Stilkenntnisse angewendet, um ein Spa zu schaffen, dessen Konturen sich vom architektonischen Idiom der Zwischenkriegszeit und jenen Häusern ableiten lassen, die der Fantasie Le Corbusiers entsprangen. • Heinz Legler et Véronique Lièvre ont puisé à nouveau dans leurs connaissances approfondies des styles pour créer un spa dont la silhouette s'inspire directement de l'idiome architectural de l'Interbellum et des maisons nées de l'imagination de Le Corbusier.

↑ The treatment-building and the stairs in hewn stone form a striking contrast. • Der Kontrast zwischen dem Haus für Körperpflege und der zum Meer hinabführenden Treppe aus rohem Stein ist augenfällig. • Le contraste entre le bâtiment des soins et l'escalier en pierre brut qui descend vers la mer est saisissant.

→ In this discreetly luxurious establishment, specialists devote themselves to the corporeal benefit of the guests and the staff wear immaculate white clothing. • In diesem, einem diskreten Luxus verpflichteten Betrieb, in dem sich Fachkräfte ganz um das körperliche Wohlbefinden der Gäste kümmern, ist makelloses Weiß Pflicht. • Dans cet établissement d'un luxe discret où des spécialistes se consacrent entièrement au bien-être corporel des hôtes, le blanc immaculé est de rigueur

← The open-air shower with its duck-board floor is protected from prying eyes by a lattice-work screen and hidden in an alcove of the terrace. • Die mit einem Gitterrost am Boden ausgestattete Dusche im Freien, von einem Vorhang aus Latten gegen indiskrete Blicke abgeschirmt, schmiegt sich an eine Auskleidung der Terrassenwand. • La douche en plein air avec son plancher en caillebottis se protège des regards indiscrets par la présence d'un écran en lattes de bois et se love dans un renfoncement de la terrasse.

PP. 242–243 On the semi-circular grand terrace, seats and a table in untreated wood
invite one to relax and contemplate the oceanic vista. • Auf der großen, halbkreisförmig angelegten Terrasse laden ein Tisch und Sitze aus rohem Holz zur Entspannung und zu einem kontemplativen Blick auf die endlose Weite des Meeres ein. • Sur la grande terrasse construite en demi-cercle, des sièges et une table en bois brut invitent à la détente et à la contemplation d'une mer qui s'étend à perte de vue.

P. 246 At the heart of this pale sky-blue building, a bed awaits those who have come to be treated with extracts of papaya, avocado and coconut. •
In diesem, in blassblauer Himmelsfarbe gehaltenen Gebäude wartet ein Bett auf Gäste, die sich eine Massage mit Extrakten aus Papayas, Avocados und Kokosnüssen gönnen. • Au cœur de ce bâtiment couleur de ciel pâle, un lit attend celui ou celle qui viendra se procurer des soins à base d'extraits de papaye, d'avocat et de noix de coco.

P. 247 In the Verana Day Spa, the smallest object or piece of furniture becomes a work of art. • Jedes einzelne Möbel, jedes einzelne Objekt wird im Verana Day Spa zu einem Kunstwerk. • Dans le Verana Day Spa, le moindre meuble et le moindre objet deviennent œuvres d'art.

PP. 248–249 A rectangular opening in a wall becomes a veritable seascape. To be massaged by expert hands in front of a spectacular view is an unforgettable experience. • Eine rechteckige Öffnung in der Wand wirkt fast wie ein lebendiges Bild. Sich bei einem derart spektakulären Ausblick von erfahrenen Händen massieren zu lassen, ist ein unvergessliches Erlebnis. • Une découpe rectangulaire dans un mur devient un véritable tableau. Se faire masser par des mains habiles face à une vue spectaculaire est une expérience inoubliable.

↑ The "Zen" atmosphere of the place extends to the smallest details and the eye glides with undiluted pleasure over the still lifes constituted by a few bottles and a table inspired by the curved form of a tribal stool. • Die Zen-Atmosphäre des Hauses ist an kleinsten Details abzulesen. Mit Vergnügen streift der Blick jedes noch so schlichte Stillleben, wie dieses aus Flakons und einem Tischchen in der Art eines afrikanischen Hockers. • L'ambiance « zen » du lieu se lit dans le moindre détail et le regard caresse avec plaisir la plus simple des natures mortes composée avec quelques flacons et un table inspirée par la forme incurvée d'un tabouret tribal.

→ A shallow bowl in stone filled with shells testifies to Heinz and Véronique's taste for sober and refined compositions. • Eine mit Muscheln gefüllte Schale aus Stein, auf den Sims eines Fensters gestellt, zeugt von Heinz' und Véroniques Gespür für einfache, aber raffinierte Zusammenstellungen. • Une coupe en pierre remplie de coquillages posée sur le rebord d'une fenêtre reflète le goût de Heinz et Véronique pour des compositions sobres et raffinées.

HILLTOP VILLA

HILLTOP VILLA

BY DAVID HOWELL DESIGN FOR JOHN HOUSHMAND
ATOTONILCO, GUANAJUATO

Some miles outside San Miguel de Allende, the New Zealand architect David Howell has built a house named "Tierra Adentro" for the designer, sculptor and musician John Houshmand with the assistance of designer Steffani Aarons and landscape-architect Louis Franke. The materials were concrete and volcanic stone. Close to the pilgrimage shrine and World Heritage site of San Jesús Nazareno de Atotonilco (whose name means "Place of Hot Water"), the house is a haven of peace as well as an unforgettable experience for lovers of resolutely contemporary architecture.

Ein Dutzend Kilometer von San Miguel de Allende entfernt hat der neuseeländische Architekt David Howell mit Hilfe der Designerin Steffani Aarons und des Landschaftsarchitekten Louis Franke für den Designer, Bildhauer und Musiker John Houshmand ein Haus erbaut, das „Tierra Adentro" getauft wurde. Dieses Bauwerk aus Beton und vulkanischem Gestein, nahe dem Pilgerort Sankt Jesus Nazareno de Atotonilco (der „Ort der warmen Wasser" bedeutet), ist ein Refugium der Ruhe geworden und für Liebhaber konsequent zeitgenössischer Architektur ein unvergessliches Erlebnis.

À une douzaine de kilomètres de San Miguel de Allende, l'architecte neo-zélandais David Howell, assisté par la designer Steffani Aarons et l'architecte paysagiste Louis Franke, a construit une maison nommée « Tierra Adentro » pour le designer, sculpteur et musicien John Houshmand. Cette construction en béton et en pierre volcanique se trouve près du lieu de pélérinage de Saint Jesus Nazareno de Atotonilco (« Lieu des Eaux Chaudes ») ; elle est à la fois un havre de paix et une expérience inoubliable pour les amateurs d'une architecture résolument contemporaine.

PP. 252–253 Situated on nine acres of land outside the quaint artisan town of San Miguel de Allende, this modern-day hacienda has been christened "Tierra Adentro", Inner Land. • Die auf 3,6 Hektar Land außerhalb des Künstlerdorfs San Miguel de Allende gelegene moderne Hacienda wurde auf den Namen „Tierra Adentro" (Inneres Land) getauft. • Occupant 3,6 hectares près de la ville coloniale de San Miguel de Allende, un centre d'artisanat, cette hacienda moderne est baptisée « Tierra Adentro » (ou Terre intérieure).

P. 255 David Howell used the architecture to frame views, as here in this inner courtyard. The exterior façades are surfaced with tinted stucco. • Wie hier in diesem Innenhof zu sehen, setzte David Howell die Architektur zur Einrahmung von Aussichten ein. Die Fassaden sind mit getöntem Putz versehen. • David Howell a intégré des ouvertures dans l'architecture afin d'encadrer des paysages, comme ici dans cette cour intérieure. Les façades ont été enduites d'un stuc teinté.

← On the rooftop terrace, Sunbrella acrylic was used to upholster the banquette cushions. • Die Polsterkissen auf der Sitzbank der Dachterrasse wurden mit Sunbrella-Outdoorstoff bezogen. • Sur le toit-terrasse, les coussins des banquettes ont été tapissés de toiles acryliques Sunbrella.

PP. 258–259 A painting by Marion Perlet, a Canadian artist who lives in San Miguel, hangs on one of the rough plaster living room walls. • An einer der grob verputzten Wände des Wohnzimmers hängt ein Gemälde von Marion Perlet, einer kanadischen Künstlerin, die in San Miguel lebt. • Un tableau de Marion Perlet, une artiste canadienne vivant à San Miguel, orne l'un des murs du séjour laissé en plâtre brut.

↑ The house is surrounded by lush and brilliantly coloured landscaping. Grass grows between the stone pavers, mesquite trees sway in the breeze and boulders act as sculptural elements around the pool. • Das Haus ist von einer üppig bepflanzten Gartenanlage in prächtigen Farben umgeben. Zwischen Steinplatten wächst Gras, Mesquite-Bäume wiegen sich im Wind, und Felsblöcke fungieren als skulpturale Elemente rund um den Pool. • La maison est entourée d'un jardin paysagé luxuriant et coloré. Des graminées poussent entre les dalles en pierre, des prosopis ondoient dans le vent et des rochers forment des sculptures autour de la piscine.

→ In the main dining room, local chairs flank a willow dining table designed by Houshmand. He also created the wrought-iron chandelier in collaboration with Steffani Aarons. • Im großen Esszimmer flankieren lokal gefertigte Stühle einen Esstisch aus Weide, der von Houshmand designt wurde. Zusammen mit Steffani Aarons schuf er auch die gusseiserne Kerzenleuchte. • Dans la salle à manger principale, des chaises locales entourent une table créée par Houshmand. Il a également conçu le lustre en fer forgé en collaboration avec Steffani Aarons.

PP. 262–263 A brick "boveda" ceiling, terracotta floors and a custom concrete tub and wash-basin in the combined master bath and lounge. Vintage sofas flank a John Houshmand maple table. • Eine „Boveda"-Gewölbedecke aus Ziegeln, Terrakottaboden und eine maßgefertigte Badewanne sowie ein Waschtisch aus Beton befinden sich in dem Raum, der als Lounge und Bad dient. Zwei Vintage-Sofas flankieren einen niedrigen Tisch von John Houshmand. • Dans ce salon et salle de bains, un plafond voûté en « boveda », un sol carrelé en terre cuite, une baignoire et des vasques en béton réalisées sur mesure. Deux canapés vintage flanquent une table basse en érable de John Houshmand.

↑ Traditional Mexican masks hang on the dining room wall. The candleholder was made by a local tinsmith. • Traditionelle mexikanische Masken hängen an der Wand im Esszimmer. Der Kerzenleuchter wurde von einem lokalen Schmied gefertigt. • Des masques traditionnels mexicains au mur de la salle à manger. Le chandelier a été réalisé par un ferblantier local.

→ A snug nook carved out of volcanic stone is the perfect spot for a siesta. • Die gemütliche, mit Lavasteinen gestaltete Ecke ist der perfekte Ort für eine Siesta. • L'alcôve en pierres volcaniques est idéale pour la sieste.

P. 266 Mesquite stools stand in front of the glazed ceramic kitchen counter. The steel pendant is custom-made. • Stühle aus Mesquite-Holz vor der gefliesten Küchentheke. Die Hängeleuchte aus Stahl ist maßgefertigt. • Des tabourets en prosopis devant le comptoir de cuisine en céramique émaillée. Le plafonnier en acier a été réalisé sur mesure.

P. 267 Local handblown glasses and terracotta vases in the sunflower-yellow kitchen. • Lokale mundgeblasene Gläser und Terrakottavasen in der sonnengelben Küche. • Dans la cuisine jaune tournesol, des vases locaux en verre soufflé et terre cuite.

↑ Vibrant Mexican bed covers in the children's guest room. • Tagesdecken in kräftigem Grün im Kinder-Gästezimmer. • Dans la chambre d'amis des enfants, des dessus-de-lit mexicains aux couleurs vives.

→ In this guest bathroom, cast-concrete fixtures are offset by the warmth of mesquite wood and a bright wool rug. • Die Betoneinbauten im Gästebad kontrastieren mit dem Waschtisch aus Mesquite-Holz und dem bunten Wollteppich. • Dans cette salle de bains pour amis, l'équipement en béton moulé contraste avec la chaleur du meuble sous-vasque en prosopis et du tapis en laine vivement coloré.

HOTELITO DESCONOCIDO

HOTELITO DESCONOCIDO

PUERTO VALLARTA

The Hotelito Desconocido is that rare creature of the resort world – a harmonious balance of luxury and ecological purity, pampering and primitive beauty, set amid a wetland preserve for sea turtles and 150 species of birds. Nestled along the Costa Alegre, between the Pacific Ocean and the Sierra Madre Mountains (60 miles south of Puerto Vallarta), the solar-powered Hotelito was conceived by Marcello Murzilli as a place to celebrate rather than contain nature. It is built along the lines of an old Mexican fishing village, and the 29 accommodations in rooms and suites are in simple but lovely palafitos – airy bungalows built on stilts to overlook the edge of the estuary. After a day of riding horses along the beach or biking through palm groves, an al fresco aromatherapy massage or stone therapy (alternating warm river rocks with cool marble stones) soothes stressed muscles. And the restorative Mermaid Bath draws upon local ingredients – sea salts and botanical essential oils – to smooth away dead skin, cleanse toxins, and massage skin back to a natural glow.

Das Hotelito Desconocido schafft nicht nur den Spagat zwischen Luxus und Umweltbewusstsein, verschwenderischen Pflegeprogrammen und natürlicher Schönheit, sondern liegt außerdem mitten in einem Naturschutzgebiet für Meeresschildkröten und 150 Vogelarten. Das komplett mit Sonnenenergie betriebene Hotelito schmiegt sich zwischen Pazifik und Sierra Madre (100 Kilometer südlich von Puerto Vallarta) an die Costa Alegre. Konzipiert wurde es von Marcello Murzilli, der einen Ort schaffen wollte, an dem man der Natur huldigt, anstatt sie zu zähmen. Diese Anlage mit 29 Zimmern und Suiten besteht aus schlichten, aber umso hübscheren „Palafitos" – geräumigen Bungalows, von denen aus man den Meeresarm überblickt. Wer den Tag mit Ausritten am Strand oder Radtouren durch die Palmenhaine verbracht hat, freut sich auf eine Aromatherapie-Massage im Freien. Oder aber man genießt eine Massage, bei der abwechselnd warme Flusskiesel und kühler Marmor eingesetzt werden, um verhärtete Muskeln zu entspannen. Beim erholsamen Meerjungfrau-Bad kommen ausschließlich einheimische Zutaten wie Meersalze und essenzielle Pflanzenöle zum Zug, die abgestorbene Hautschuppen entfernen, den Körper entgiften und die Haut durch eine Massage wieder zum Strahlen bringen.

L'hôtel Desconocido est une rareté dans le monde des hôtels. Niché dans un écrin de nature, véritable sanctuaire aquatique abritant tortues de mer et quelques 150 espèces protégées d'oiseaux, l'établissement offre un équilibre harmonieux entre luxe hôtelier et préservation de l'écosystème, entre soins haut de gamme et beauté brute de la nature. Construit sur la Costa Alegre, entre l'océan Pacifique et les montagnes de la Sierra Madre (à moins de 100 kilomètres au sud de Puerto Vallarta), l'Hotelito, alimenté par l'énergie solaire, fut conçu par Marcello Murzilli. À l'emplacement d'un ancien village de pêcheurs, ses appartements avec 29 chambres et suites sont de simples mais coquets bungalows sur pilotis – les « palafitos » – dominant les rives de l'estuaire. Après une randonnée à cheval le long de la plage ou une excursion à vélo à travers les palmeraies, les tensions musculaires disparaîtront sous l'effet bienfaisant d'un massage aux huiles essentielles ou d'une séance de « stone therapy » (applications alternées de galets chauds et de pierres de marbre froides). Le revigorant Bain de la sirène fait appel aux ingrédients indigènes, comme des sels marins et des huiles essentielles à base de plantes locales, pour éliminer les peaux mortes et les toxines, et masser la peau en douceur pour lui redonner son éclat naturel.

HARAMARA RETREAT

HARAMARA RETREAT

NAYARIT

How many shades of green are there? How does the green of the grasses, bushes, ferns and the pine forests on the mountain crests on the horizon disappear into the white-blue of the sky, merging from there into the turquoise-blue of the sea, and transform itself from the grey-brown of the forgotten rocks on the beach into the golden yellow of the sand? Wherever you look at the Haramara Retreat, colours explode. The yoga sessions in the yoga pavilion that is open 360 degrees and stands high on the hill are an adventure in themselves. A fabulous view onto the entangled jungle all about you comes as the reward after intense practice. If the thicket in your own head has not been wonderfully cleared after that, Vipassana meditation is a possibility. Or simply the luxury of a good old-fashioned midday nap. When the sky hovers hot over Haramara, time stands still for a couple of hours. And the spirit finds peace. If you haven't booked one of the world-class massages, wild horses couldn't drag you from the hand-woven linen of the romantic and charmingly furnished bungalows. Only the whales—also in evidence here, by the way—might just manage it.

Wie viele Schattierungen von Grün gibt es? Wie taucht das Grün der Gräser, Sträucher, Farne, der Kiefernwälder auf den Bergkämmen am Horizont ins weißliche Blaue des Himmels, von dort ins Türkisblau des Meers – und verwandelt sich vom Graubraun der am Strand vergessenen Felsbrocken ins Goldgelbe des Sandes? Wohin auch immer man blickt im Haramara Retreat, es explodieren Farben. Ein Abenteuer für sich sind die Yogastunden in dem rundum offenen Yogapavillon, der einen Hügel bekrönt. Ein sagenhafter Ausblick auf den verknoteten Dschungel ringsum ist die Belohnung nach intensivem Üben. Wenn sich danach das Dickicht im eigenen Kopf nicht auf wundersame Weise löst, gibt es die Möglichkeit zur Vipassana-Meditation – oder einfach den Luxus einer altmodischen Mittagsruhe. Spätestens dann, wenn der Himmel heiß über Haramara schwebt, bleibt für ein paar Stunden die Zeit stehen, und der Geist findet Ruhe. Hätte man nicht eine der Weltklasse-Massagen gebucht, würden einen keine zehn Pferde von den handgewebten Laken in den romantisch-charmant eingerichteten Bungalows trennen können. Höchstens Wale. Die gibt es hier nämlich auch.

Combien de tons de vert existe-t-il ? Comment le vert des herbes, buissons, fougères et forêts de pins sur les cimes montagneuses à l'horizon se fond-il au bleu pâle du ciel, puis dans le bleu turquoise de la mer, avant de passer du gris brun des rochers oubliés sur la plage au jaune doré du sable ? Au Hamarara Retreat, où que le regard se pose, les couleurs explosent. Les séances de yoga, véritables événements, ont lieu dans le pavillon de yoga ouvert à 360 degrés qui trône tout en haut de la colline. Une splendide vue panoramique sur la forêt vierge enchevêtrée tout autour est la récompense après un entraînement intensif. Si, après cela, la jungle de l'esprit n'est toujours pas défrichée, une méditation Vipassana est possible. Ou tout simplement le luxe d'une sieste classique. Au plus tard à cet instant-là, tandis que le ciel brûlant plane au-dessus de Hamarara, le temps s'arrête pour quelques heures. Et l'esprit trouve la paix. Si l'on n'était pas inscrit à l'un des massages haut de gamme, rien ne pourrait vous tirer des toiles de lin tissées main des charmants bungalows romantiques. Tout au plus des baleines. Parce qu'il y en a ici aussi.

PP. 274–275 In the Haramara Retreat the roofs of the bungalows take the form of pointed hats; they raise their heads above the luxuriant vegetation like giant mushrooms. • Die Bungalow-Dächer im Haramara Retreat haben die Form spitz zulaufender Hüte. So, wie sie aus der üppigen Vegetation hervorragen, wirken sie wie riesige Pilze. • Dans le Haramara Retreat les toits des bungalows ont pris la forme d'un chapeau pointu et la façon dont ils pointent la tête dans la végétation abondante les fait ressembler à des champignons géants.

P. 277 After a session of Yoga or Vipassana meditation, how wonderful to stretch out on the sand in the protective shade of an awning thatched with palm leaves. Beyond the rocks lies the sea and we hear the soothing rhythm of its waves. • Nach Yoga-Übungen oder einer Vipassana-Meditation tut es gut, sich am Strand im schützenden Schatten eines mit Palmenblättern gedeckten Vordachs auszuruhen. Gleich hinter den Felsen rauscht im entspannenden Rhythmus seiner Wellen das Meer. • Après une séance de Yoga ou une méditation Vipassana il fait bon se reposer sur le sable dans l'ombre protectrice d'un auvent coiffé de feuilles de palmier. Au-delà des rochers il y la mer et le rythme relaxant des vagues.

PP. 278–279 Under the impressive dome of the palapa Yoga Pavilion, it is difficult to tear one's eyes away from the endless 360-degree view. • Es ist nicht einfach, unter der eindrucksvollen Kuppel des Palmdachs, das den Yoga-Pavillon bedeckt, den Blick nicht schweifen und sich während der Übungen nicht von einem Rundumblick in die unendliche Weite ablenken zu lassen. • Sous le dôme impressionnant de la palapa qui coiffe le Pavillon de Yoga il est difficile de détourner le regard et de ne pas se laisser distraire pendant la séance par une vue panoramique de 360 degrés qui s'étend à perte de vue.

← The balconies of the bungalows have been furnished with a table and chairs in the best Mexican craft traditions. What could be better to enjoy a beautiful view of the landscape and a magnificent sunset? • Die Balkons der Bungalows wurden mit Tischen und Sesseln in bester mexikanischer Handwerkstradition möbliert. Ein Grund mehr, den schönen Blick auf die Landschaft oder den wunderbaren Sonnenuntergang zu genießen. • Les balcons des bungalows ont été meublés avec une table et des fauteuils dans la meilleure tradition artisanale mexicaine. Raison de plus pour profiter d'une belle vue sur le paysage ou d'un magnifique coucher de soleil.

↓ The outdoor shower is protected by a curved red screen that looks like a giant shell. • Die Dusche im Freien wird von einer roten, eingebuchteten Schutzwand abgeschirmt, die wie eine riesenhafte Muschel aussieht. • La douche en plein air est protégée par un écran rouge incurvé qui ressemble à une coquille géante.

PP. 282–283 Open-sided, this palapa becomes a sunshade and harbours a sumptuous en-suite. With its twin beds and matching mosquito nets, it guarantees perfect repose in a dream-like décor. • Die mit Dächern aus Palmblättern gedeckten und nach allen Seiten hin offenen Bungalows sind wie ein Sonnenschirm und weiten sich zugleich zu einer luxuriösen Suite. Ausgestattet mit Doppelbetten und dazu passenden Moskitonetzen garantieren sie vollständige Ruhe in traumhafter Umgebung. • Ouverte à tous les vents, la palapa devient ombrelle et offre le gîte à une suite somptueuse. Équipée avec des lits jumeaux et leurs moustiquaires assorties, elle garantit un repos absolu dans un décor de rêve.

ENDÉMICO

ENDÉMICO

VALLE DE GUADALUPE

Scattered loosely across the hillside as if they'd tumbled from the back of a speeding truck, the twenty cabins of Endémico in Valle de Guadalupe are raised up on stilts that make them look like individual lookout posts. The prospects thus afforded to guests are surprisingly attractive –the barren hills contrasting starkly with the carpet of grapevines covering the fertile valley floor. The bottled results of the latter can be sampled on the terrace of your wooden cube—after a couple of glasses under the Mexican sun, you'll be even more taken with this experimental hotel. Its steel-and-wood eco-cabins are both functional and aesthetic, the main building houses a bar and a restaurant, and there's also a glorious pool with far-reaching views. Wind and weather, it is hoped, will soon age the facades, ensuring they are even better integrated into the landscape—thus making this the perfect hideaway for travelers who like to blend in.

Als hätte ein Laster in den Hügeln des Valle de Guadalupe seine Ladung verloren, so verstreut stehen die 20 Holzkabinen im Gelände. Jede Kabine ist auf ihren Stelzenfüßen ein eigener Aussichtsposten, wobei der Ausblick von den kargen Höhen überraschend bekömmlich ist – Weinstöcke bedecken den fruchtbaren Boden des gesamten Tals. Was da heranreift, kann gleich auf der Holzterrasse vor dem Wohnwürfel verkostet werden, und spätestens beim zweiten Glas Wein unter der Sonne Mexikos wird man zugeben müssen, dass dieses Hotelexperiment äußerst zufriedenstellend verläuft. Das Eco-Design der kleinen Häuser aus Stahl und Holz ist ebenso funktional wie ansprechend, im Hauptgebäude warten Bar und Restaurant, und einen herrlichen Pool mit Fernsicht gibt's auch. Die Betreiber hoffen, dass Wind und Wetter die Fassaden der Kabinen bald verwittern lassen, damit sie perfekt mit der Umgebung verschmelzen. Zur Freude aller, die im Urlaub nicht auffallen möchten.

À la manière d'un chargement tombé d'un camion, les vingt cabanes de bois sont éparpillées dans les collines de la vallée de Guadalupe. Montées sur pilotis, elles offrent des points d'observation uniques sur le paysage. D'ailleurs, vu des hauteurs arides, le panorama est étonnamment amène : des pieds de vigne tapissent le sol fertile de la vallée. Ce qui mûrit ici peut être aussitôt savouré sur la terrasse en bois du logement cubique. Et au deuxième verre de vin sous le soleil du Mexique, force est de reconnaître que cette expérience hôtelière est très réussie. L'écoconception de ces maisonnettes de bois et de métal est aussi fonctionnelle que séduisante. Le bâtiment principal abrite un bar et un restaurant ; il y a aussi une superbe piscine avec vue dégagée. Les hôteliers espèrent que les intempéries patineront les façades tant et si bien qu'elles se fondront dans le paysage, pour le plaisir de ceux qui veulent passer inaperçus en vacances.

PP. 284–285 Scattered through the untouched landscape of the immense valley of Guadalupe, the twenty little cabins on stilts have been built in a combination of wood and metal and their surprising shapes form an ensemble of striking beauty. The swimming pool commands an astounding panorama and can indeed boast of offering guests a "pool with a view". • Die überraschenden Umrisse der 20 über die unberührte Landschaft des Tals von Guadalupe verteilten, auf Pfeilern ruhenden und aus Holz und Metall erbauten Hütten bilden ein Ensemble von ungewöhnlicher Schönheit. Vom hochgelegenen Schwimmbad aus eröffnet sich ein umwerfendes Panorama. Es bietet den Gästen ein regelrechtes „Bad mit Ausblick". • Parsemées dans le paysage vierge de l'immense vallée de Guadalupe, les vingt cabanes sur pilotis ont été construites en mariant le bois et le métal et leurs silhouettes surprenantes forment un ensemble d'une beauté insolite. La piscine surplombe un panorama époustouflant et elle peut se vanter d'offrir aux hôtes un véritable « bain avec vue ».

P. 287 On the terraces looking down over the pool and rocks, designer furniture with a "vintage" look ensures the guests' comfort. • Designermöbel vom Typ „Vintage" sorgen auf den Terrassen oberhalb des Schwimmbads für den nötigen Komfort. • Sur les terrasses qui dominent la piscine et les rochers, un mobilier design de type « vintage » se charge du confort nécessaire.

PP. 288–289 Each cabin's wooden deck comes with a traditional Mexican clay stove, allowing guests to enjoy a fireside glass of wine in the open air. • Jede der Wohnkabinen hat einen Freisitz mit traditionellem mexikanischem Lehmofen – für moderne Lagerfeuerstimmung bei einem Glas Wein vor dem Zubettgehen. • Chaque terrasse dispose d'un foyer traditionnel mexicain en argile permettant de déguster un verre de vin au coin du feu avant d'aller au lit.

↖ In this strange, arid landscape, the outdoor bar, admirable in its austerity – it is made of wooden planks and a metal frame – is the ideal meeting point for guests in search of relaxation. • In dieser trockenen und ungewöhnlichen Landschaft ist die bewusst schlicht gehaltene, aus Holzplanken und Metallgestellen gebaute Bar im Freien ein idealer Treffpunkt für Gäste, die sich entspannen wollen. • Dans ce paysage aride et hors du commun, le bar en plein air, sobre à souhait, construit avec des planches en bois et une armature en métal est le point de rencontre idéal pour les hôtes en quête de détente.

↑ The futuristic look of the cabins is a splendid match for the "lunar" aspect of the landscape and at night the chimeneas on the terraces sparkle like the stars. • Das futuristische Erscheinungsbild der Hütten fügt sich perfekt in die „Mondlandschaft" des Tales ein. Abends flimmert die Glut der Kohleöfen und oben funkeln die Sterne. • L'aspect futuriste des cabanes sied à merveille au paysage « lunaire » de la vallée et, le soir, les braseros sur les terrasses scintillent dans la nuit et font écho aux étoiles.

PP. 292–293 There is a striking contrast between the cabins and the landscape around them; the austere linear decoration of the light-walled bedrooms emphasizes the strange beauty of the Gaudalupe valley. • Der Kontrast zwischen der Inneneinrichtung der Hütten und der umgebenden Landschaft ist erstaunlich. Die sachlich-klare Ausstattung der Zimmer mit ihren hellen Wänden hebt die sonderbare Schönheit des Tals von Guadalupe hervor. • Le contraste entre l'intérieur des cabanes et le paysage environnant est saisissant et la décoration dépouillée et graphique des chambre aux parois clairs accentue la beauté étrange de la vallée de Guadalupe.

PRODUIT DE LA REPUBLIQUE POPULAIRE DE CHINE
ARBOUSES AU SIROP LEGER
La fábula

A COLLECTOR'S PASSION

A COLLECTOR'S PASSION

MANOLO RIVERO CERVERA
MÉRIDA

Manolo Rivero Cervera adopted the British expression "living above the shop" when it came to setting up his apartment above the Hotel Trinidad and his gallery. Rivero, who thus combines work and private life with the greatest of ease, is fired by a veritable passion for contemporary art. And he has proved his own talents as an artist and creator, putting together the most eclectic collection of paintings, furniture and objets d'art without ever committing the sin of bad taste or kitsch. Rivero's home is not recommended to those insensitive to the 20th-century charms of Pop Art, Op Art, Hyperrealism and Surrealism, nor to those whose aesthetic senses may be shocked by the daring juxtaposition of a 'rocaille' sofa and scattering of Versace cushions with an Art Nouveau statuette and the lurid tones of a contemporary canvas. Just for the record, Julian Schnabel swears by Rivero's taste and a New York gallery will soon stage an exhibit of his work. Meanwhile, guests at the Hotel Trinidad are enchanted by the magical atmosphere of this Aladdin's cave.

„Living about the shop" – dieser typisch englische Ausdruck passt auf Manolo Rivero Cervera, der sich über seinem Hotel Trinidad und seiner Galerie eine Wohnung eingerichtet hat und so Berufs- und Privatleben in Einklang bringt. Es ist schon beeindruckend, wie leidenschaftlich Rivero sich für die zeitgenössische Kunst interessiert, welches Talent als Künstler und Gestalter er entfaltet und mit welch sicherer Hand er die verschiedensten Objekte, Möbel und Gemälde kombiniert, ohne in schlechten Geschmack oder gar Kitsch abzugleiten. Gegnern der Pop-Art, Op-Art, des Hyperrealismus oder des Surrealismus, kurz: der Kunst des 20. Jahrhunderts, ist von einem Besuch bei Rivero abzuraten. Das Gleiche gilt für jene, die vor der gewagten Zusammenstellung eines Rokokosofas mit einer Jugendstilstatuette, Kissen à la Versace und einem zeitgenössischen Gemälde in kräftigen Farben zurückschrecken. In Riveros „Höhle" wimmelt es von solchen Referenzen. Erwähnt sei, dass Julian Schnabel ganz und gar auf diesen Geschmack schwört, dass Riveros eigene Bilder bald in einer New Yorker Galerie gezeigt werden und dass die Hotelgäste von dem charmanten Kunterbunt begeistert sind.

« Living about the shop » – cette expression typiquement britannique illustre bien la situation de Manolo Rivero Cervera qui a installé son appartement au-dessus de son hôtel Trinidad et de sa galerie, réussissant ainsi parfaitement à marier travail et vie privée. Rivero impressionne par sa passion pour l'art contemporain, son talent comme artiste et créateur et sa capacité à marier les objets, les meubles et les tableaux les plus divers sans tomber dans le mauvais goût et le kitsch. Évidemment, rendre visite à Rivero n'est pas recommandé à ceux qui sont réfractaires au pop art, op art, hyperréalisme, surréalisme – en bref à l'art du 20e siècle, ni à ceux que la juxtaposition osée d'un canapé rocaille, d'une statuette Art nouveau, de quelques coussins à la Versace et d'un tableau contemporain aux vives couleurs fait frissonner d'horreur. La « caverne » de Rivero est remplie de références. Mentionnons que Julian Schnabel ne jure que par son goût, qu'une galerie de New York exposera bientôt ses propres œuvres et que les clients de son hôtel sont enchantés de ce merveilleux capharnaüm.

PP. 294–295 Rivero has put together a bold personal collection in his residence. A giant canvas by José Bedia hangs alongside works by Jean-Paul Souchaud. • In seiner Wohnung hat Rivero einfach alles zusammengetragen, was er liebt. Ein großes Gemälde von José Bedia wird von Werken von Jean-Paul Souchaud flankiert. • Dans sa demeure, Rivero a assemblé avec audace ce qu'il aime. Un grand tableau de José Bedia est flanqué par des œuvres de Jean-Paul Souchaud.

← and P. 297 The pool is only a few steps away from the gallery that leads to the salon filled with an impressive array of artwork and other treasures. • Vom Swimmingpool sind es nur ein paar Schritte zur Galerie, die in den Salon führt, in dem sich zahlreiche Kunstwerke und Fundstücke aller Art befinden. • Quelques pas seulement séparent la piscine de la galerie qui mène au salon abritant de nombreuses œuvres d'art et des trouvailles en tout genre.

↑ Enshrined in a corner alcove, this carved wooden saint is decorated with a gilded crown and bedecked with antique rosary beads. • Die in einer Nische ausgestellte Heiligenfigur aus Holz erhielt eine goldene Krone und wurde mit alten Rosenkränzen geschmückt. • Une sainte en bois sculpté, exposée dans une niche, est coiffée d'une couronne dorée et décorée avec des chapelets anciens.

↑ Song of the siren. The master of the house has wrought his art on this Barbie doll, transforming her into a fish-tailed mermaid perched atop a towel rail in the bathroom. • Die Barbiepuppe auf dem Handtuchhalter des Badezimmers hat der Hausherr in eine Sirene verwandelt. • Une Barbie transformée en sirène singulière signée par le maître de maison est posée sur le porte-serviettes de la salle de bains.

→ Rivero's works, exhibited in one of the rooms of the private gallery, bear witness to his own great talent as an artist. • Riveros eigene Arbeiten, die in einem Raum seiner Galerie ausgestellt sind, belegen sein künstlerisches Talent. • Les œuvres de Rivero exposées dans l'une des salles de sa galerie privée témoignent de son talent d'artiste.

NO PIENSE
NO EN ARTE

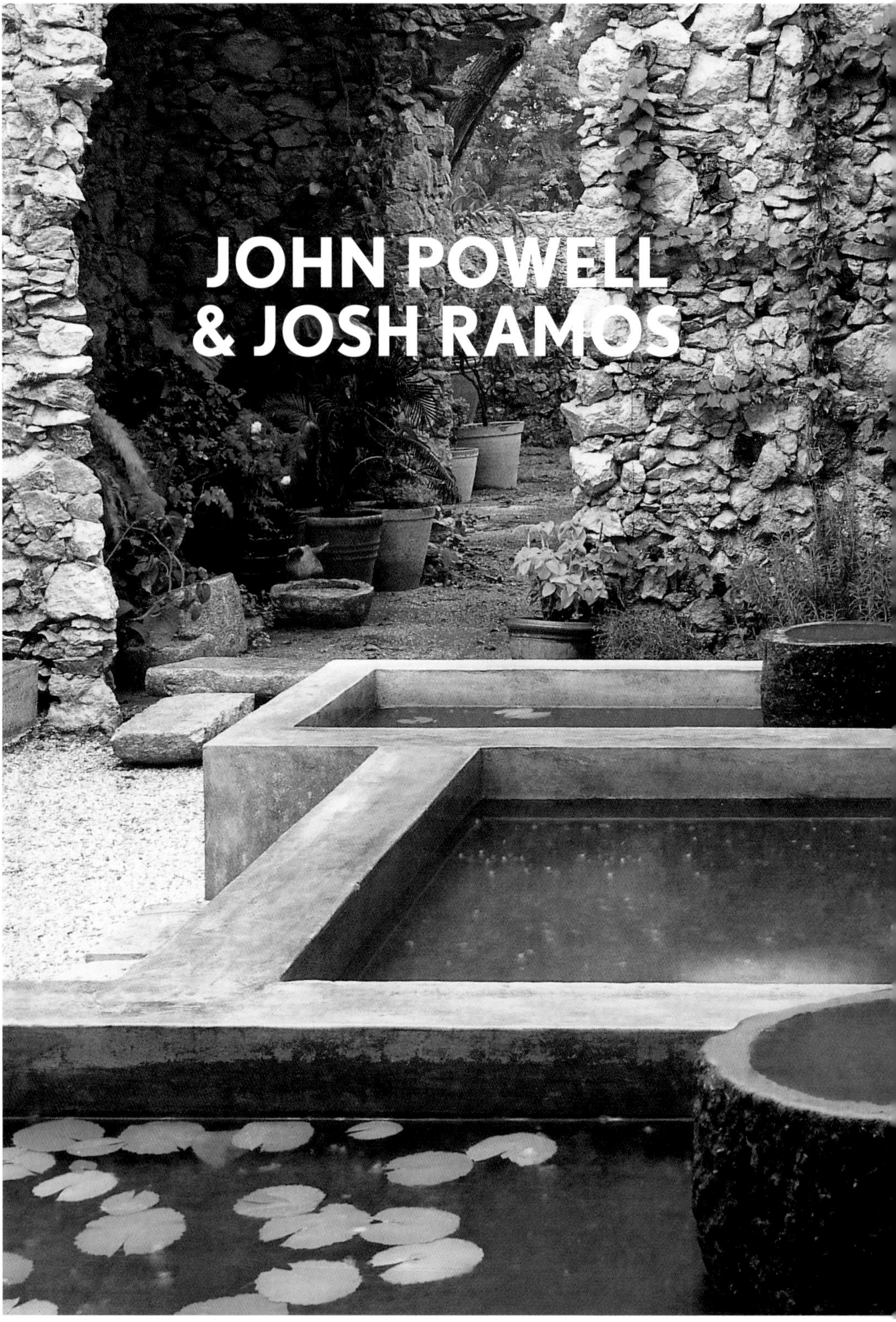
JOHN POWELL
& JOSH RAMOS

JOHN POWELL & JOSH RAMOS

MÉRIDA

The Ermita de Santa Isabel is one of the oldest neighbourhoods in Mérida. And John Powell and Josh Ramos, who saved one of its four-centuries-old dwellings from destruction, can be thankful they began restoration work on the roof. Without that, they say, their home would never have withstood the ferocious storms that rage through the Yucatán on a regular basis. John Powell has enjoyed a multifarious career as an artistic director, painter, décor and costume designer, interior decorator, antiques dealer and fashion model. He has also worked as an assistant to John Saladino, Stephen Sills and Hervé Van der Straeten. When Powell bought his home with partner Josh Ramos, a painter and fabric designer who works for many of the top fashion houses in Europe, Mexico and the U.S., the couple undertook eight exhausting months of restoration. Now, two years on, the oldest part of the quinta is filled with the couple's tasteful finds, resplendent with antique furniture, exquisite artwork and sacred objects. Thanks to their boundless energy and ideas, these two talented artists have breathed fascinating new life into an ancient abode.

Ermita de Santa Isabel gehört zu den ältesten Stadtvierteln von Mérida und John Powell und Josh Ramos haben dort ein 400 Jahre altes Haus vor der Zerstörung bewahrt. Sie sind froh, bei der Restaurierung mit dem Dach begonnen zu haben, andernfalls, so glauben sie, hätte der Bau einen jener verheerenden Stürme, die in regelmäßigen Abständen über Yucatán hinwegfegen, nicht überstanden. John war in seinem Leben wechselweise Artdirector, Maler, Bühnen- und Kostümbildner, Antiquar und Model. Außerdem hat er als Assistent von John Saladino, Stephen Sills und Hervé van der Straeten gearbeitet. Als John gemeinsam mit seinem Partner Josh Ramos, ebenfalls Maler und Stoffdesigner für namhafte Firmen in Europa, Mexiko und den USA, das Haus in Mérida erwarb, hatten die beiden mit enormen Problemen zu kämpfen und acht Monate aufreibende Restaurierungsarbeiten vor sich. Zwei Jahre nach dem ersten Spatenstich ist der älteste Trakt der Quinta mit passenden Fundstücken, schönen alten Möbeln, Kunstwerken und sakralen Kunstobjekten eingerichtet. Mit ihrem Ideenreichtum und ihrer Energie haben die beiden Künstler ihm ein faszinierendes Gesicht verliehen.

L'Ermita de Santa Isabel est l'un des plus vieux quartiers de Mérida, et John Powell et Josh Ramos qui y ont sauvé in extremis une maison de quatre siècles se félicitent d'avoir commencé par la restauration du toit. Selon eux, la demeure n'aurait pas résisté à une des tempêtes dévastatrices qui soufflent régulièrement sur le Yucatán. John a été tour à tour directeur artistique, peintre, créateur de décors et de costumes, décorateur, antiquaire et mannequin. Il a aussi été l'assistant de John Saladino, Stephen Sills et Hervé Van der Straeten. En achetant cette maison à Mérida avec son partenaire Josh Ramos, lui-même peintre et qui crée des tissus pour des maisons renommées en Europe, au Mexique et aux États-Unis, John a dû affronter d'énormes problèmes et huit mois de restauration épuisante. Deux ans après le premier coup de pioche, la partie la plus ancienne de la quinta est remplie de trouvailles heureuses, de beaux meubles anciens, d'œuvres d'art et d'objets d'art sacré. Les deux artistes pleins d'idées et d'énergie lui ont donné un visage fascinant.

PP. 302–303 John and Josh have made an interesting feature of the ruined walls around the courtyard: the pool and the water-lily filled ponds they built themselves. • In dem von ruinenhaften Mauern umgebenen Hof haben John und Josh ein Schwimmbecken und Seerosenteiche angelegt. • John et Josh ont su tirer le meilleur parti des murs en ruines qui entourent la cour, la piscine et les bassins aux nénuphars construits par leurs soins.

P. 305 The rustic benches and Medici vase in the entrance hall give visitors a foretaste of the house's pure, simple décor. • Im Eingangsbereich geben die rustikale Bank und eine Medici-Vase einen Vorgeschmack auf die schlichte Einrichtung. • Dans l'entrée, des bancs rustiques et un vase Médicis donnent un avant-goût de la sobriété du décor.

↑ Throughout the house there are still lifes composed by the owners, testifying to their instinctive tastes for interior decoration. • Überall im Haus sind von den Hausherrn zusammengestellte Stillleben zu entdecken. Sie zeugen von ihrem instinktiven Gespür für Inneneinrichtung. • Partout dans la maison, on découvre des natures mortes composées par les maîtres de maison. Elles témoignent de leurs gouts instinctifs pour la décoration intérieure.

→ The former designer and the antique dealer have both marked the house with their sense of style. • Im gesamten Haus erkennt man die Handschrift des früheren Designers und des Antiquars. • Le goût des deux artistes pour les formes et les antiquités sont perceptibles dans chaque pièce.

PP. 308–309 The simple forms of the rustic furniture in the dining room transform it into a window onto the past. • Die bäuerlichen Möbel des Esszimmers mit ihren schlichten Formen lassen den Raum zu einem Fenster in die Vergangenheit werden. • Dans la salle à manger, le mobilier campagnard aux formes simples et rustiques transforme la pièce en une fenêtre sur le passé.

← The "18th-century"-style baldachin stands central in the master bedroom. Its very simple metal frame has no need of the flowing curtains with which it would once have been hung. • Das Bett mit einem Baldachin im Stil des 18. Jahrhunderts nimmt im Schlafzimmer der Hausherrn den gebührenden Platz ein. Das sehr klar konturierte Metallgestell kann auf überflüssige Vorhänge verzichten. • Le lit à baldaquin de style « dix-huitième » occupe une place importante dans la chambre à coucher du maître de maison. Son armature en métal très graphique se passe bien d'un habillement de rideaux superflus.

↑ Perched on top of a chest in the entrance hall, this colourful saint welcomes visitors on arrival. • Auf einer Truhe im Vestibül empfängt eine farbige Heiligenfigur die Besucher. • Posé sur un bahut du vestibule, un saint haut en couleurs accueille les visiteurs.

↑ A detail of the stone, stucco and marble shower cubicle built by John Powell and Josh Ramos. • Die Duschkabine aus Stein, Stuck und Marmor ist von den Hausherrn selbst gebaut. • Un détail de la cabine de douche en pierre, stuc et marbre construite par les maîtres de maison.

→ The shower room – the height of unadorned simplicity and understated chic. • Das Badezimmer – schnörkellos schlicht. • La salle d'eau – toute de sobriété et de dépouillement.

SALVADOR REYES RIOS & JOSEFINA LARRAIN LAGOS

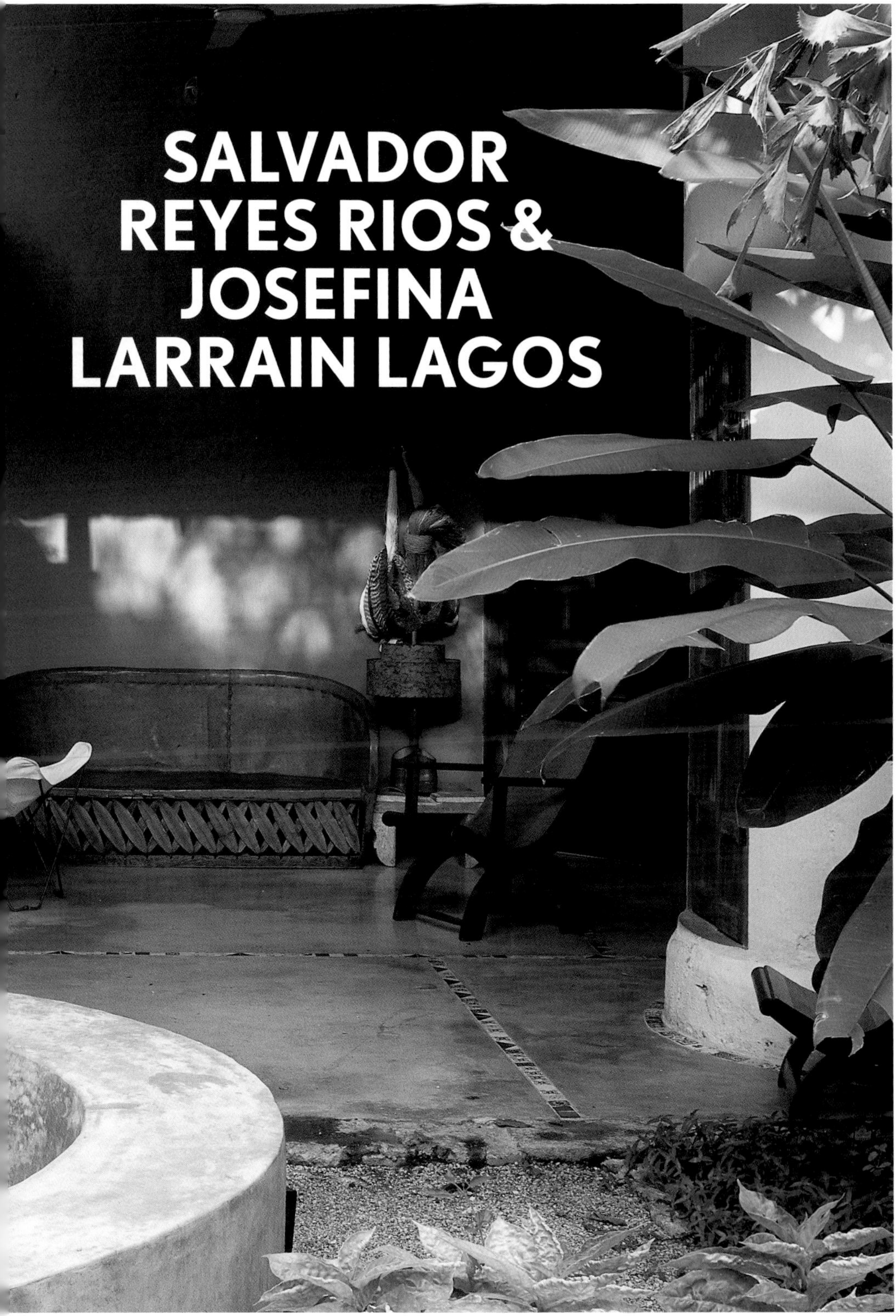

SALVADOR REYES RIOS & JOSEFINA LARRAIN LAGOS

MÉRIDA

The streets of Yucatán's capital are a treasure trove of colonial architecture. Eyes never grow weary of contemplating late 19th-century wonders such as the Paseo de Montejo, lined with ornate stucco-decorated palaces and cut through with numbered alleyways filled with brightly coloured houses. The renowned Mexican architect Salvador Reyes Rios and his wife, designer Josefina Larrain Lagos, live here with their two children in a low-rise residence adorned with classical pilasters. Salvador and Josefina have restructured their turn-of-the-century home, giving it a resolutely contemporary feel, but their modern makeover integrates several historical features, such as cement flagstones and a beautiful colonnade leading onto the patio. The couple's pure tastes have also influenced the interiors. They have maintained a rustic spirit in the kitchen, a sober but comfortable style in the bathroom and decorated their home with stylishly minimalist furniture throughout. Their remarkable metamorphosis is completed with eye-catching details such as a striking section of blue wall, a strelitzia arranged in a vase and an elegant bathtub placed in the middle of the garden.

Wer in der Hauptstadt von Yucatán spazieren geht, kann die Schätze der Kolonialarchitektur Ende des 19. Jahrhunderts bewundern. Immer und immer wieder lässt man die Blicke über den Paseo de Montejo schweifen. Viele mit Stuck verzierte Paläste stehen dort, und ordentlich nummerierte Gassen, in denen sich Häuser in leuchtenden Farben reihen, kreuzen ihn. Salvador Reyes Rios, ein bekannter Architekt, und seine Frau, die Designerin Josefina Larrain Lagos, bewohnen mit ihren beiden Kindern ein recht niedriges Haus, das mit klassischen Pfeilern geschmückt ist. Unter Erhaltung einiger Details dieser Epoche wie der Zementfliesen und des Säulengangs zum Patio haben die Besitzer die Räumlichkeiten jenseits der Toreinfahrt völlig neu gegliedert und diesem Haus aus der Jahrhundertwende ein entschieden modernes Ambiente verliehen. Auch das Interieur verrät den Wunsch nach Einfachheit. Das Paar hat die rustikale Küche behalten, ein komfortabel-funktionales Badezimmer eingerichtet und Möbel von mustergültiger Schlichtheit ausgesucht. Ein blauer Mauerabschnitt, eine Strelitzie in einer Vase und eine Badewanne im Garten vervollständigen diese bemerkenswerte Metamorphose.

Se promener dans la capitale du Yucatán, c'est pouvoir admirer des trésors de l'architecture coloniale de la fin du 19e siècle. On ne se lasse pas de contempler le Paseo de Montejo bordé de palais décorés de « pâtisseries » en stuc et traversé de ruelles dûment numérotées où s'alignent des maisons aux couleurs vives. Salvador Reyes Rios, un architecte connu, et son épouse Josefina Larrain Lagos, designer, habitent avec leurs deux enfants une maison assez basse ornée de pilastres classiques. Au-delà de l'entrée cochère, les maîtres des lieux ont restructuré les espaces tout en gardant quelques détails d'époque comme les dalles de ciment et la colonnade qui donne accès au patio. Ils ont conféré à cette demeure fin de siècle une ambiance résolument contemporaine. L'intérieur montre le même souci de simplicité. Le couple a gardé la cuisine rustique, créé une salle de bains dépouillée et confortable et choisi des meubles d'une sobriété exemplaire. Un pan de mur bleu, un strelitzia dans un vase et une baignoire au milieu du jardin complètent cette métamorphose remarquable.

PP. 314–315 The patio at the Reyes Rios residence extends into a leafy green garden which may not be vast, but where else would you find such a stylish outdoor bath? • An den Hof des Hauses von Salvador Reyes Rios und seiner Familie schließt sich ein kleiner Garten an. Dort steht eine Freiluftbadewanne aus Stein. • Dans la maison des Reyes Rios, le patio est prolongé par un jardin de dimensions modestes mais qui abrite une baignoire en plein air.

P. 317 When siesta time approaches, dream your dreams in the deep blue depths of the patio. • Während der Siesta kann man im Blau des Patios herrlich träumen. • À l'heure de la sieste, on peut rêver dans le bleu du patio.

PP. 318–319 A canopy is draped above the paved courtyard, providing shade from the sun. • Ein Sonnensegel schützt den gepflasterten Hof vor der Mittagshitze. • Un vélum protège la cour pavée du grand soleil.

↑ Interior shutters and wire meshing provide a cool retreat from the Mexican sun. In the narrow passageway near the dining room a slender cactus tapers towards the ceiling. • Die sich nach innen öffnenden Fensterläden sorgen für angenehme Kühle. Im schmalen Durchgang am Esszimmer ragt schlank ein Kaktus auf. • Les volets intérieurs et les grillages dispensent une fraîcheur agréable. Un étroit passage près de la salle à manger abrite un cactus élancé.

→ The owners have kept original design features in the kitchen, such as the traditional Mexican tilework and the impressive chimney hood. • In der Küche sind die traditionelle mexikanische Kachelung und der großzügig bemessene Rauchfang erhalten geblieben. • La cuisine a conservé son carrelage traditionnel mexicain et sa hotte aux dimensions généreuses.

↑ The wicker lamp, designed by Josefina Larrain Lagos, echoes the lines of the patio columns. • Die von der Hausherrin entworfene Leuchte aus Korbweide harmoniert ausgezeichnet mit den Säulen im Hof. • Le luminaire en osier tressé conçu par la maîtresse de maison est en parfaite harmonie avec les colonnes du patio.

→ A strelitzia cuts a striking silhouette against the vivid blue background of the patio wall. • Die schmale Silhouette einer Strelitzie hebt sich vom kräftigen Blau des Patios ab. • La silhouette acérée d'un strelitzia se découpe sur le mur bleu vif du patio.

PP. 324–325 The furniture Salvador Reyes Rios designed for the living room reflects this architect's love of pure, clean lines. The overhead skylight built into the ceiling makes clever use of natural light. • Im Wohnzimmer kündet das vom Architekten selbst entworfene Mobiliar von seiner Vorliebe für klare Formen. Das Licht fällt durch einen geschickt in die Decke eingelassenen Dachreiter. • Dans le séjour, le mobilier dessiné par l'architecte reflète sa prédilection pour les lignes pures. La lumière zénithale provient d'un lanterneau habilement intégré au plafond.

↑ The bed, inspired by the design of late 18th-century "pencil posts", was designed by the architect. • Das Bett im „Pencil Post"-Stil des ausgehenden 18. Jahrhunderts ist ein Entwurf des Architekten. • Le lit, inspiré des « pencil post » de la fin du 18e siècle, porte la signature de l'architecte.

→ Salvador and Josefina's bathroom was decorated by the architect with admirably simple furniture. The traditional tiling ensures the coolness of the room and facilitates maintenance. • Das Badezimmer von Salvador und Josefina wurde vom Hausherrn mit Mobiliar von beispielhafter Schlichtheit ausgestattet. Die traditionellen Fliesen auf dem Boden gewähren eine angenehme Kühle und sind zugleich pflegeleicht. • La salle de bains de Salvador et Josefina a été décorée par l'architecte avec un mobilier d'une simplicité exemplaire. La présence d'un carrelage traditionnel garantit une fraîcheur agréable et une facilité d'entretien.

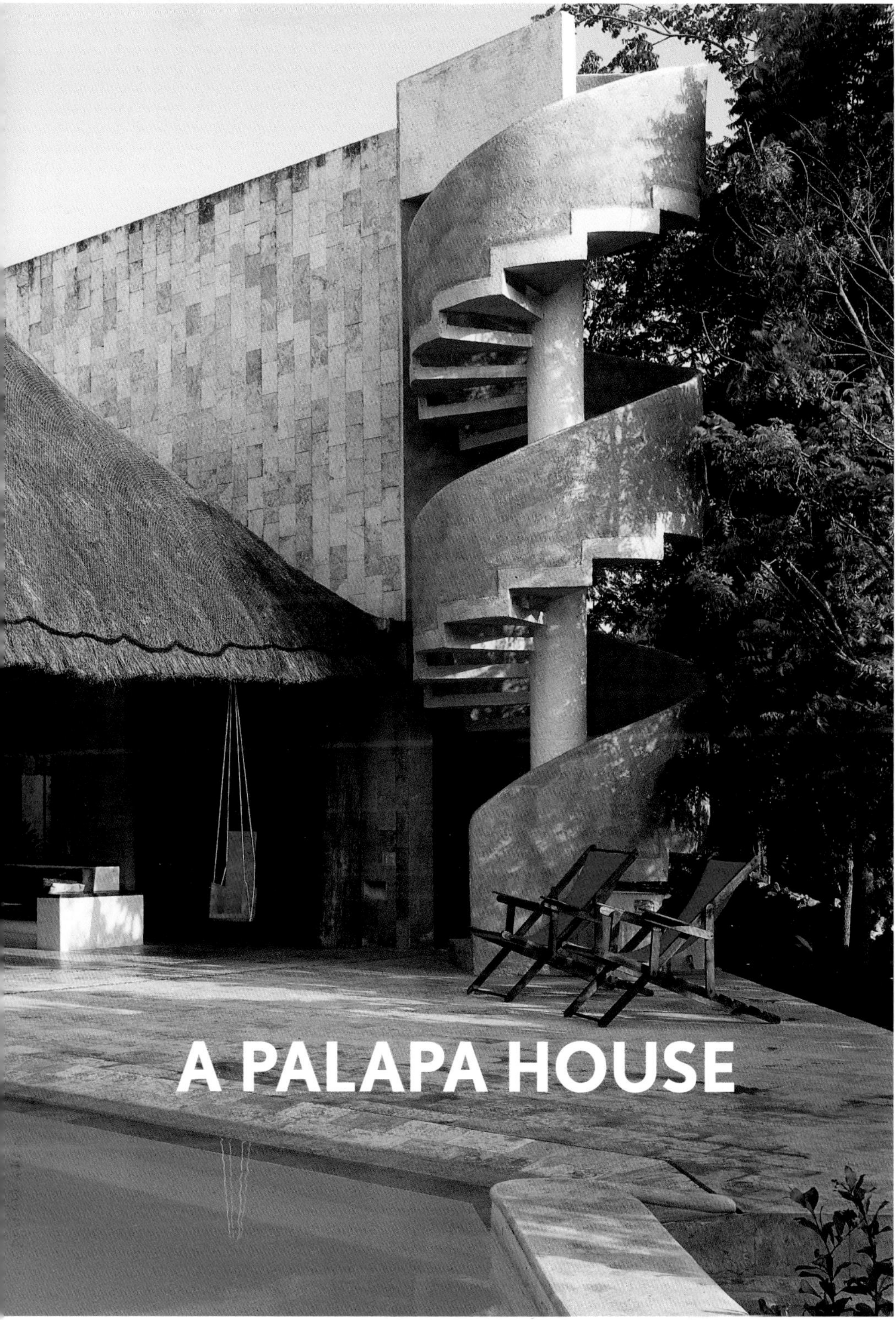

A PALAPA HOUSE

A PALAPA HOUSE

JOSEFINA ESPEJO
MÉRIDA

Coming upon Colonia La Ceiba, visitors will be pleasantly surprised by the characteristic charms of this residential neighbourhood in Mérida and impressed by the wide variety of forms, architectural styles and eye-catching colours. From a Le Corbusier-style villa and a residence influenced by the palette and minimalism of Luis Barragán to a sturdy house where natural materials and neutral tones dominate, a host of different architects have let their creative imagination run riot. And you can understand why Josefina Espejo and her architects Luis Torres Perazza and Alvaro Ponce Espejo chose to experiment with something a little out of the ordinary, too. Josefina, whose main aim was to create a cool and light-filled family home, "open to the four winds," adopted the form of the traditional palapa. The result is a spacious, open-sided dwelling with a thatched roof that looks out onto terraces, a Californian-style pool and a second palapa, housing a dining area and a children's play area. A truly original way of living and communing with nature.

Nähert man sich der Colonia La Ceiba, einem Residenzviertel am Rande von Mérida, so ist man angenehm überrascht von der ausgesprochen charaktervollen Erscheinung des Bauensembles. Eine Vielzahl von Stilen, einladenden Formen und Farben beherrschen das Bild – von der Villa im Stil Le Corbusiers über ein Wohnhaus, das sich an die Strenge und Farbgebung Luis Barragáns hält, bis zum robusten Landhaus mit natürlichen Baustoffen und neutralen Tönen. Der Erfindungsgeist der verschiedenen Architekten ist beeindruckend, und man versteht sofort, weshalb Josefina Espejo und ihre Architekten Luis Torres Perazza und Alvaro Ponce Espejo ebenfalls beschlossen haben, neue Wege zu gehen. Mit dem Ziel, ein helles, kühles und nach allen Seiten offenes Einfamilienhaus zu bauen, hat Josefina die Form einer traditionellen Palapa gewählt. Heute öffnet sich dieses große, mit Stroh gedeckte Sonnendach auf verschiedene Terrassen, einen Swimmingpool im kalifornischen Stil und eine weitere Palapa, in der sich ein Essbereich und Spielflächen für die Kinder befinden. Eine originelle und angenehme Art, im Freien zu leben.

En s'approchant de la Colonia La Ceiba, un quartier résidentiel aux confins de Mérida, le visiteur est agréablement surpris par l'aspect très caractéristique de l'ensemble et par une grande variété de styles, de formes et de couleurs attrayantes. De la villa style Le Corbusier à la demeure influencée par la rigueur et la palette de Barragán, en passant par la robuste maison où dominent les matériaux naturels et les teintes neutres, on est séduit par l'esprit inventif des différents architectes. Et l'on comprend pourquoi Josefina Espejo et ses architectes Luis Torres Perazza et Alvaro Ponce Espejo ont choisi à leur tour de quitter les sentiers battus. Soucieux de créer une maison de famille lumineuse, fraîche et « ouverte à tous les vents », Josefina a adopté la forme de la palapa traditionnelle. Aujourd'hui, ce grand parasol coiffé de chaume s'ouvre sur des terrasses, une piscine californienne et une autre palapa qui abrite un restaurant et des aires de jeux pour les enfants. Une façon originale et agréable de vivre en plein air.

PP. 328–329 Minimalist contemporary architecture merges with the traditional form of the palapa. • Die sachlichen Umrisse zeitgenössischer Architektur gehen eine raffinierte Verbindung mit der traditionellen Palapa ein. • Les lignes sobres de l'architecture contemporaine sont astucieusement mariées à celles de la palapa traditionnelle.

P. 331 An artistically positioned tree trunk by the pool serves as a piece of contemporary sculpture. • Der Baumstamm neben dem Schwimmbad wirkt wie eine moderne Skulptur. • Près de la piscine, un tronc d'arbre fait office de sculpture contemporaine.

← Hidden amongst a sway of banana trees and towering palms, this paradisiacal palapa makes the perfect outdoor living and dining room. • Von Bananenstauden und Palmen umgeben, dient die hübsche Palapa als Wohn- und Esszimmer im Freien. • La magnifique palapa entourée de bananiers et de palmiers sert de séjour et de salle à manger en plein air.

↑ Built in pure Mexican style, the car port belies its true nature. Only close observation reveals its true function as a garage. • Jedes Detail des im reinsten mexikanischen Stils gebauten Carports verleugnet seine eigentliche Funktion. • Chaque détail du « car port » construit dans le plus pur style mexicain dément sa vraie fonction.

↑ On a table composed of a pair of tree trunks and a wooden top, the folkloric Mexican carved-wood candle-holders form an agreeable and eye-catching ensemble. • Auf einem Tisch, der sich aus zwei Baumstümpfen und einer Holzplatte zusammensetzt, bilden zwei typisch mexikanische Barock-Kerzenleuchter aus geschnitztem Holz ein schön anzusehendes Ensemble, das den Blick auf sich zieht. • Sur une table qui se compose d'une paire de troncs d'arbres et d'une tablette en bois, des chandeliers baroques en bois sculpté, typiquement mexicains, forment un ensemble agréable qui attire le regard.

→ Children love to play in this second, smaller palapa built at the bottom of the garden. • Eine zweite, bescheidenere Palapa wurde im hinteren Teil des Gartens errichtet. Die Kinder spielen dort besonders gern. • Une seconde palapa, plus modeste, a été édifiée au fond du jardin. Les enfants adorent y jouer.

↑ Gnarled tree trunks form a natural colonnade, separating the entrance from the inner courtyard and the car port. • Mächtige Baumstämme bilden eine Art Kolonnade, die den Eingangsbereich von Innenhof und Carport trennt. • De gros troncs d'arbre forment la colonnade qui sépare l'entrée de la cour intérieure et de l'abri à voitures.

→ Framed against the red ochre walls of a small courtyard, a sapling spreads its branches in the sun. • In dem kleinen rötlich ocker getünchten Hof streckt ein junger Baum seine Äste der Sonne entgegen. • Dans une petite cour aux murs badigeonnés d'ocre rouge, un jeune arbre tend ses branches vers le soleil.

HACIENDA XCUMPICH

HACIENDA XCUMPICH

SYLVIANE BOUCHER LE LANDAIS
MÉRIDA

The Xcumpich, a magnificent hacienda dating back to the latter half of the 19th-century, lies just north of Mérida. The hacienda's "casa principal" is secluded behind a high stone wall, which protects the house's blood-red façade, imposing portico and neoclassical columns from passing eyes. When Sylviane Boucher Le Landais, the famous French archaeologist and Mayan ceramics specialist, bought the Xcumpich in 1984, this historically important house was a pile of ruins. Following Sylviane through this splendid residence today, it is hard to imagine the sheer extent of rebuilding and restructuring work it required. The main living room (the former "sala") on the garden side of the house has been embellished with a gallery of thick columns. And its immaculate whiteness makes a dramatic contrast with the deep red of the entrance and the warm golden yellow of the dining room. Traditional furniture and folkloric objects are played off against the house's simple architecture elsewhere. In the lush green garden a fountain adorned with smiling cherubs plays, its tranquil splashing the only sound in this oasis of quiet beauty.

Die „Casa Principal" der Hacienda Xcumpich, die im Norden von Mérida liegt und aus der zweiten Hälfte des 19. Jahrhunderts stammt, ist von einer hohen Mauer umgeben, hinter der sich eine blutrote Fassade, großzügige Proportionen, ein imposanter Portikus und klassizistische Säulen verbergen. Als die gebürtige Französin Sylviane Boucher Le Landais, eine angesehene Archäologin und Spezialistin für Maya-Keramiken, 1984 die Hacienda kaufte, standen von dem einst so wunderbaren Gebäude nur noch Ruinen. Wer heute als Besucher mit Sylviane durch die Räume geht, kann sich den Umfang der geleisteten Arbeiten kaum vorstellen. Das große Wohnzimmer, die frühere „Sala", liegt zum Garten und wird heute durch eine Galerie mit stabilen Säulen verschönert. Die makellosen Weißtöne kontrastieren mit dem tiefen Rot des Eingangsbereichs und dem Goldgelb des Esszimmers. Traditionelle Möbel und volkskunstliche Objekte ergänzen die schnörkellose Architektur perfekt. Im Garten plätschert ein mit pausbäckigen Cherubinen verzierter Springbrunnen, der Xcumpich zu einer Oase der Schönheit werden lässt.

La « casa principal » de l'Hacienda Xcumpich, située au nord de Mérida et qui date de la seconde moitie du 19e siècle, est entourée d'un haut mur qui dissimule sa façade couleur sang de bœuf et ses proportions généreuses, son portique imposant et ses colonnes néoclassiques. Lorsque Sylviane Boucher Le Landais, Française de naissance, archéologue renommée et spécialiste des céramiques mayas, l'a acquise en 1984, il ne restait plus que ruines de cette maison au passé prestigieux. En suivant aujourd'hui Sylviane à travers la demeure, le visiteur peut difficilement s'imaginer l'ampleur des travaux accomplis. Le grand salon (l'ancienne « sala ») côté jardin a été embelli par une galerie aux robustes colonnes. Sa blancheur immaculée contraste avec le rouge soutenu de l'entrée et le jaune doré de la salle à manger ; les meubles traditionnels et des objets populaires se marient parfaitement à l'architecture dépouillée. Dans le jardin, une fontaine couronnée de chérubins joufflus murmure sur un fond de verdure luxuriant, faisant de Xcumpich une oasis de beauté.

PP. 338–339 Hacienda Xcumpich boasts an eye-catching façade, embellished with arches and classical columns. • Die Hacienda Xcumpich besitzt eine prächtige, mit klassischen Bögen und Säulen ausgeschmückte Fassade. • L'Hacienda Xcumpich possède une magnifique façade ornée d'arches et de colonnes classiques.

P. 341 Climb the stairs to a shady patio and an old stone fountain. • Oberhalb der Stufen erstreckt sich ein schattiger Patio mit einem alten steinernen Brunnen. • En haut des marches, un patio ombragé et une vieille fontaine en pierre.

← Like all haciendas built at the time of the "green gold" (sisal) rush, Xcumpich is a marvel of colonial architecture. • Wie alle in der Zeit des „grünen Goldes" (Sisal) erbauten Haciendas beeindruckt auch Xcumpich mit Kolonialarchitektur. • Comme toutes les haciendas construites à l'époque de l'«or vert» (sisal), Xcumpich présente une architecture coloniale impressionnante.

↑ Framed against a striking red wall, this Mexican mask fixes passers-by with its beady bird's eyes. • An einer kräftig roten Mauer fixiert eine mexikanische Maske den Besucher mit runden Vogelaugen. • Sur le mur rouge vif, un masque mexicain nous fixe de ses yeux ronds d'oiseau.

P. 344 Sylviane Boucher Le Landais is a virtuoso of the art of "less is more". She has succeeded in creating a charming decorative ensemble with nothing more than an erotic painting and a carefully chosen colour. • Sylviane Boucher Le Landais beherrscht die Kunst des „Weniger ist mehr" bis zur Perfektion. Nur mit einem Bild und einer gut gewählten Farbe gelingt es ihr, ein charmantes, dekoratives Ambiente zu schaffen. • Sylviane Boucher Le Landais maîtrise l'art du « moins, c'est plus » à la perfection et réussit à créer un ensemble décoratif charmant avec un simple tableau et une couleur bien choisie.

P. 345 All in yellow: parrot room at Hacienda Xcumpich. • Ganz in Gelb: Papageienzimmer in der Hacienda Xcumpich. • Tout en jaune : la chambre au perroquet dans l'hacienda Xcumpich.

↑ In the kitchen, the kitchen island is covered in traditional Mexican tiles and their sparkling colours impart a bright, cheerful note to the room. • Die Kochinsel in der Küche ist mit traditionellen mexikanischen Fliesen geschmückt, deren lebendige Farben dem Raum eine helle und heitere Note verleihen. • Dans la cuisine, le « potager » se couvre de carrelages mexicains traditionnels et leurs couleurs chatoyantes confèrent à la pièce une note claire et gaie.

→ A lovely bowl filled with fruit stands out against a wall of faded yellow and creates a simple but charming still life. • Eine hübsche, mit Früchten gefüllte Schale hebt sich vor einer verwaschenen gelben Wand ab. Es wirkt wie ein schlichtes, charmantes Stillleben. • Une jolie coupe remplie de fruits se détache sur un mur d'un rouge délavé et le tout forme un nature morte simple et charmante.

PP. 348–349 The rustically appointed dining room beckons lovers of Mexican cuisine, which is as tasty as it is spicy. • Im Esszimmer erwartet Liebhaber der ebenso schmackhaften wie scharfen mexikanischen Küche eine rustikale Einrichtung. • Dans la salle à manger, un robuste mobilier campagnard accueille les amateurs d'une cuisine mexicaine savoureuse et épicée.

← In the owner's bedroom, a metal construction doing duty as a baldachin combines beauty of line with perfect austerity. • Eine Metallkonstruktion, deren bewusste Einfachheit sich mit schlichter Schönheit paart, deutet ein Baldachinbett an. • Dans la chambre de la maîtresse de maison, une construction en métal qui allie le souci du dépouillement à la beauté linéaire fait office de lit à baldaquin.

↑ An indefatigable collector of charming objects, Sylviane arranges her finds on the walls of her home with admirable flair. • Sylviane, eine unermüdliche Sammlerin reizvoller Objekte, hängt ihre Fundstücke mit einem untrüglichen Gespür an den Wänden ihres Wohnsitzes auf. • Collectionneuse infatigable d'objets de charme, Sylviane accroche ses trouvailles sur les murs de sa demeure avec un flair remarquable.

← In the guest room the eye is drawn to the very beautiful floor of diagonally-laid square tiles. • Auffällig ist der mit sehr schönen, rautenförmigen Fliesen bedeckte Boden im Gästezimmer. Das schmiedeeiserne Bett verleiht dem Ambiente zudem eine romantische Note. • Un sol couvert d'un très beau carrelage retient l'attention dans la chambre d'amis. Le lit en fer forgé ajoute une note romantique.

↑ A Mexican bathroom must be cool and full of light and this washroom at the Hacienda Xcumpich is no exception. • Hell und kühl sollen Badezimmer in Mexiko sein, die Waschräume der Hacienda Xcumpich machen da keine Ausnahme. • Au Mexique, les salles de bains se doivent d'être claires et fraîches et la salle d'ablutions de la Hacienda Xcumpich ne fait pas exception à règle.

HACIENDA POXILA

HACIENDA POXILA

ALEJANDRO PATRÓN LAVIADA
MÉRIDA

The Hacienda Poxila stands on the Camino Real, a road linking Mérida to Campeche, a fortress on the west coast of Yucatán that was pillaged and destroyed by French, English and Dutch pirates. Like most of the other important estancias in the region, the Poxila partly dates back to the 16th-century. The hacienda thrived under its owner, maize producer Lorenzo Mateo Caldera, in the 18th-century, but enjoyed a veritable golden age in the next thanks to the cultivation of sisal. Under the management of the Lara family, the Poxila went on to become the impressive neoclassical residence it is today. Like all haciendas in Yucatán, the Poxila is made up of a sumptuous master's house, a machine room and a number of smaller outbuildings that constitute the workers' quarters. The Poxila's current owner, Alejandro Patrón Laviada, runs the place in masterly fashion and looks back on "the good old days" with a certain nostalgia. The Poxila's interiors abound with religious objects and antique furniture, while outside the lush green gardens are filled with the sound of fountains and birdsong.

Die Hacienda Poxila liegt am Camino Real, der Mérida mit Campeche verbindet, einer Festungsstadt an der Westküste von Yucatán, die von französischen, englischen und niederländischen Piraten mehrfach geplündert und geschliffen worden ist. Wie die meisten bedeutenden Estancias stammt die Anlage aus dem 16. Jahrhundert. Im 18. Jahrhundert brachte es ihr Eigentümer Lorenzo Mateo Caldera mit dem Maisanbau zu Wohlstand, ihre Blütezeit erlebte sie im 19. Jahrhundert durch die Sisalproduktion. Unter der Obhut der Familie Lara nahm Poxila die beeindruckende klassizistische Gestalt von heute an. Wie alle Haciendas in Yucatán besteht Poxila aus einem prächtigen Herrenhaus, einer Maschinenhalle und mehreren Nebengebäuden für das Personal. Der heutige Besitzer, Alejandro Patrón Laviada, leitet die Hacienda mit gelassener Autorität und beschwört gern die „gute alte Zeit" herauf. Heute stehen im Inneren wieder alte Möbel und schöne Sakralobjekte und im Garten vermischt sich das Plätschern der Springbrunnen mit dem Gezwitscher der Vögel.

L'Hacienda Poxila se trouve sur le Camino Real qui relie Mérida à Campeche, une forteresse située sur la côte ouest du Yucatán et qui fut pillée et détruite plusieurs fois par des pirates français, anglais et hollandais. Elle date en partie du 16e siècle, comme la plupart des plus importantes estancias. Au 18e siècle, elle s'est enrichie sous son propriétaire Lorenzo Mateo Caldera, producteur de maïs, mais c'est au 19e siècle qu'elle a connu son âge d'or avec le sisal. Gérée par la famille Lara, Poxila est devenue le bâtiment impressionnant d'aspect néoclassique que l'on connaît aujourd'hui. Comme toutes les haciendas du Yucatán, Poxila est composée d'une somptueuse maison de maître, d'une salle des machines et de plusieurs dépendances pour le personnel. L'actuel propriétaire, Alejandro Patrón Laviada, dirige l'hacienda de main de maître et sait évoquer le « bon vieux temps ». Aujourd'hui, les intérieurs abritent à nouveau des meubles anciens et de beaux objets religieux, et, dans les jardins verdoyants, le murmure des fontaines se marie aux cris des oiseaux.

PP. 354–355 Thanks to the passion and unswerving determination of its owner the Hacienda Poxila has maintained its imposing architecture. • Mit Enthusiasmus und Einsatz rettete der neue Eigentümer die ebenso sachliche wie eindrucksvolle Architektur der Hacienda. • L'architecture sobre et impressionnante de l'Hacienda Poxila a été sauvée par l'enthousiasme et les efforts de son propriétaire.

P. 357 The brick-coloured stucco façades of the workers' former living quarters and the machine room have been left unaltered. • Die frühere Dienstbotenwohnung und die Maschinenhalle haben ihre mit ziegelrotem Gips verputzten Fassaden behalten. • L'ancien logis du personnel et la salle des machines ont gardé leurs façades enduites de stuc couleur brique.

↑ The centennial walls of the Poxila have been eroded by the elements and their venerable aspect is eloquent of the house's prestigious past. • Die alten Mauern von Poxila sind von den Elementen gezeichnet, doch diese Spuren der Vergangenheit erzählen auch von glanzvollen Zeiten. • Les anciens murs de Poxila sont rongés par les éléments et leur aspect vétuste raconte l'histoire d'un passé prestigieux.

→ Covered passages open to the air are repositories of a rich past, full of furniture and family mementos. • Die überdachten, offenen Veranden sind mit Möbeln und Objekten vollgestellt, die die Zeiten als Familienerbe aus längst vergangenen Epochen überdauert haben. • Des passages couverts, ouvert à tous les vents, regorgent de meubles et d'objets de famille qui nous viennent d'une époque lointaine.

← In bygone days Mexican interiors were filled with religious paintings and saintly icons. Alejandro Patrón Laviada has recreated this holy atmosphere in his 21st-century home. • Früher fanden sich in den mexikanischen Innenräumen zahlreiche Heiligenbilder und -statuen. Alejandro Patrón Laviada hat es verstanden, diese von aufrichtigem Glaubensgefühl geprägte Atmosphäre wieder herzustellen. • Autrefois, les intérieurs mexicains abritaient de nombreux tableaux et statues de saints. Alejandro Patrón Laviada a su reconstituer cette ambiance imprégnée d'un sentiment religieux sincère.

↑ A polychrome wooden sculpture from the 18th-century presents an irresistibly charming infant Jesus, all pink and chubby. • Eine aus dem 18. Jahrhundert stammende Skulptur aus mehrfarbigem Holz stellt ein rosiges, pausbäckiges Jesuskind dar, dessen Reize entzücken. • Une sculpture en bois polychrome datant du 18e siècle représente un petit Jésus rose et joufflu au charme irrésistible.

PP. 362–363 The 19th-century furniture in the master bedroom, where vast spaces echo like a ballroom, harks back to a golden age of charm and prosperity. A Virgin and child cast protective glances over the bed • Im Hauptschlafzimmer, weitläufig wie ein Ballsaal, erinnert das Mobiliar aus dem 19. Jahrhundert an eine glanzvolle Zeit. Eine Madonna mit Kind hängt über dem Kopfende des Bettes. • Dans la chambre maîtresse, vaste comme une salle de bal, le mobilier 19e évoque une époque prospère et pleine de charme. Une Vierge à l'enfant domine la tête de lit.

THE NOBLE HORSE

↑ A 19th-century wooden cross leans against a wall daubed in yellow ochre. • Nahe dem Eingang ein Holzkreuz aus dem 19. Jahrhundert vor einer ockergelb getünchten Mauer. • Près de l'entrée, une croix en bois du 19e siècle devant un mur badigeonné d'ocre jaune.

→ A heart-shaped candle-holder in the private chapel is still bedecked with religious candles and votive offerings. • Nach wie vor ist die Privatkapelle ein Raum der Andacht mit Kerzen in dem herzförmigen Kandelaber. • Dans la chapelle privée, le porte-cierges en forme de cœur accueille toujours les bougies et les vœux d'espoir.

CASA CÁRDENAS

549

CASA CÁRDENAS

MÉRIDA

"We stumbled across Mérida and were just enchanted by it," recall Adam McCulloch and Emma Sloley. Located in the heart of the Mexican city, their house had until recently been inhabited by the same family since the late 19th-century. The couple were drawn to its tall ceilings, traditional paste-tile floors, and 65-metre-long (213 ft) lot. "One thing I wanted to preserve was that sense of distance," notes McCulloch. He oversaw the construction work and gutted about a third of the main house, adding a second story, a lap pool, and guesthouse (casita). The couple wanted the décor to be "fairly contemporary," but finding furniture locally proved tricky. "Design is a new concept for people here," remarks McCulloch, who transported the Eames chairs by plane from New York by placing the legs in a suitcase and strapping six seats at a time to his backpack. One great find they did make in Mérida is the bust of the 1930s Mexican president, Lázaro Cárdenas, whose term was a time of social reform. As Sloley recounts: "Locals coming to our house pat him on the head and say 'Hi.' "

„Wir stolperten über Mérida, und es hat uns einfach verzaubert", erinnern sich Adam McCulloch und Emma Sloley. Ihr Haus, das zuvor mehr als 100 Jahre von derselben Familie bewohnt worden war, liegt im Herzen der Stadt. Das Paar war begeistert von den hohen Decken, den traditionellen Fliesen und von dem 65 Meter langen Grundstück. „Dieses Gefühl von Weite wollte ich erhalten", sagt McCulloch, der die Bauarbeiten beaufsichtigte. Etwa ein Drittel des Hauptbaus wurde entkernt, dafür kamen ein weiteres Stockwerk, der Pool und ein Gästehaus (Casita) dazu. Die Einrichtung wünschte sich das Paar „halbwegs zeitgenössisch", doch passende Möbel vor Ort zu finden, erwies sich als schwierig. „Design ist für die Menschen hier ein neues Konzept", bemerkt McCulloch, der die Eames-Stühle im Flugzeug aus New York herbrachte, indem er ihre Beine im Koffer verstaute und je sechs Sitzschalen an seinen Rucksack schnallte. Einen großartigen Fund immerhin machten sie in Mérida: eine Büste von Lázaro Cárdenas, dem reformfreudigen mexikanischen Präsidenten der 1930er Jahre. „Wenn Einheimische uns besuchen, tätscheln sie ihm gern den Kopf und grüßen ihn", erzählt Sloley.

Située au cœur de la ville, leur maison était habitée par la même famille depuis la fin du 19e siècle. Ils ont été séduits par ses hauts plafonds, ses sols en carrelage traditionnel et son terrain de 65 m de long. « Je tenais à conserver cette impression de profondeur », explique McCulloch, qui a supervisé les travaux, évidé un tiers de la structure, ajouté un étage, un bassin de nage et une « casita » pour les amis. Le couple, qui souhaitait un décor « plutôt contemporain », a eu du mal à se meubler sur place. « Le design est un concept nouveau ici », observe McCulloch. Il a transporté ses chaises Eames depuis New York en avion en fourrant les pieds dans une valise et en arrimant les six coques sur son sac à dos. Ils ont néanmoins fait une belle trouvaille à Mérida : un buste du président Lázaro Cárdenas qui entreprit de grandes réformes sociales dans les années 1930. Sloley confie : « Quand des Mexicains nous rendent visite, ils lui donnent une tape sur la tête et le saluent. »

REIK

PP. 366–367 Measuring just 22 feet (6.7 metres) in width, the front façade is painted in the Yucatán style. • Die 6,7 Meter breite Fassade ist im Stil Yucatáns gestrichen. • La façade de seulement 6,7 m de large a été peinte dans le style du Yucatán.

P. 369 In the inner courtyard, visitors are greeted by a bronze bust of Lázaro Cárdenas, a legendary Mexican president. The couple named the house "Casa Cárdenas" for him. • Im Innenhof empfängt eine Bronzebüste von Lázaro Cárdenas, dem legendären Präsidenten Mexikos, die Besucher. Nach ihm hat das Paar das Haus „Casa Cárdenas" benannt. • Dans la cour intérieure, un buste en bronze du légendaire président mexicain Lázaro Cárdenas accueille les visiteurs. La maison a été baptisée « Casa Cárdenas » en son honneur.

PP. 370–371 On the long and narrow lot, a 27-foot (8.2-metre) lap pool was inserted between the main house and the newly built casita. • Auf dem langen und schmalen Grundstück wurde ein 8,2 Meter langer Pool zwischen Haupthaus und neu gebauter Casita eingefügt. • Un bassin de nage de 8,2 m de long a été creusé, entre la maison principale et la nouvelle « casita ».

← The couple found the plastic letters in a local store and arranged them randomly in the entry hall. Later, they discovered that "Reik" is the name of a Mexican boy band. • Das Paar fand die Plastik-Buchstaben in einem Laden vor Ort und arrangierte sie willkürlich im Vestibül. Dass „Reik" eine mexikanische Boyband ist, erfuhren sie erst später. • Les lettres en plastique disposées au hasard dans l'entrée ont été dénichées dans une boutique locale. Le couple a appris plus tard que Reik était le nom d'un boy's band mexicain.

↑ Bull-shaped piggy banks adorn the concrete kitchen shelves. • Spardosen in Gestalt von Rinderbullen defilieren auf den Küchenregalen aus Beton. • Sur les étagères en béton, une collection de taureaux-tirelires.

PP. 374–375 A vintage hacienda-style table was installed in the eat-in kitchen. The new floor tiles were laid according to the original pattern. • In der Wohnküche steht ein Vintage-Tisch im Hazienda-Stil. Die neuen Fliesen sind nach dem ursprünglichen Muster verlegt worden. • Dans la cuisine, une table ancienne de style hacienda. Le nouveau carrelage reprend les motifs du sol d'origine.

← The floor tiles and ceiling beams in the living room are original. The latter were made from unused railroad tracks in the late 1800s. • Im Wohnzimmer sind sowohl die Bodenfliesen original als auch die Deckenbalken, die Ende des 19. Jahrhunderts aus ausrangierten Eisenbahnschienen hergestellt wurden. • Le carrelage est d'origine, comme les poutres du séjour, récupérées sur des voies ferrées désaffectées à la fin du 19e siècle.

↑ The master bathroom is clad with tile and polished cement. • Das Hauptbad kleiden Mosaikfliesen und polierter Zement aus. • La salle de bains principale, en carrelage et béton poli.

PP. 378–379 The 1930s chair with cane seat in Sloley's study is the type that locals still take out onto curbs in the evening to catch up on the daily gossip. • Der Sessel mit Flechtsitz in Sloleys Büro ist aus den 1930er Jahren. Auf solchen Stühlen setzen sich die Einheimischen noch immer zum abendlichen Plausch vor ihre Häuser. • La chaise cannée des années 1930 dans le bureau de Sloley ressemble à celles que les gens du quartier sortent sur le trottoir le soir pour s'informer des derniers potins.

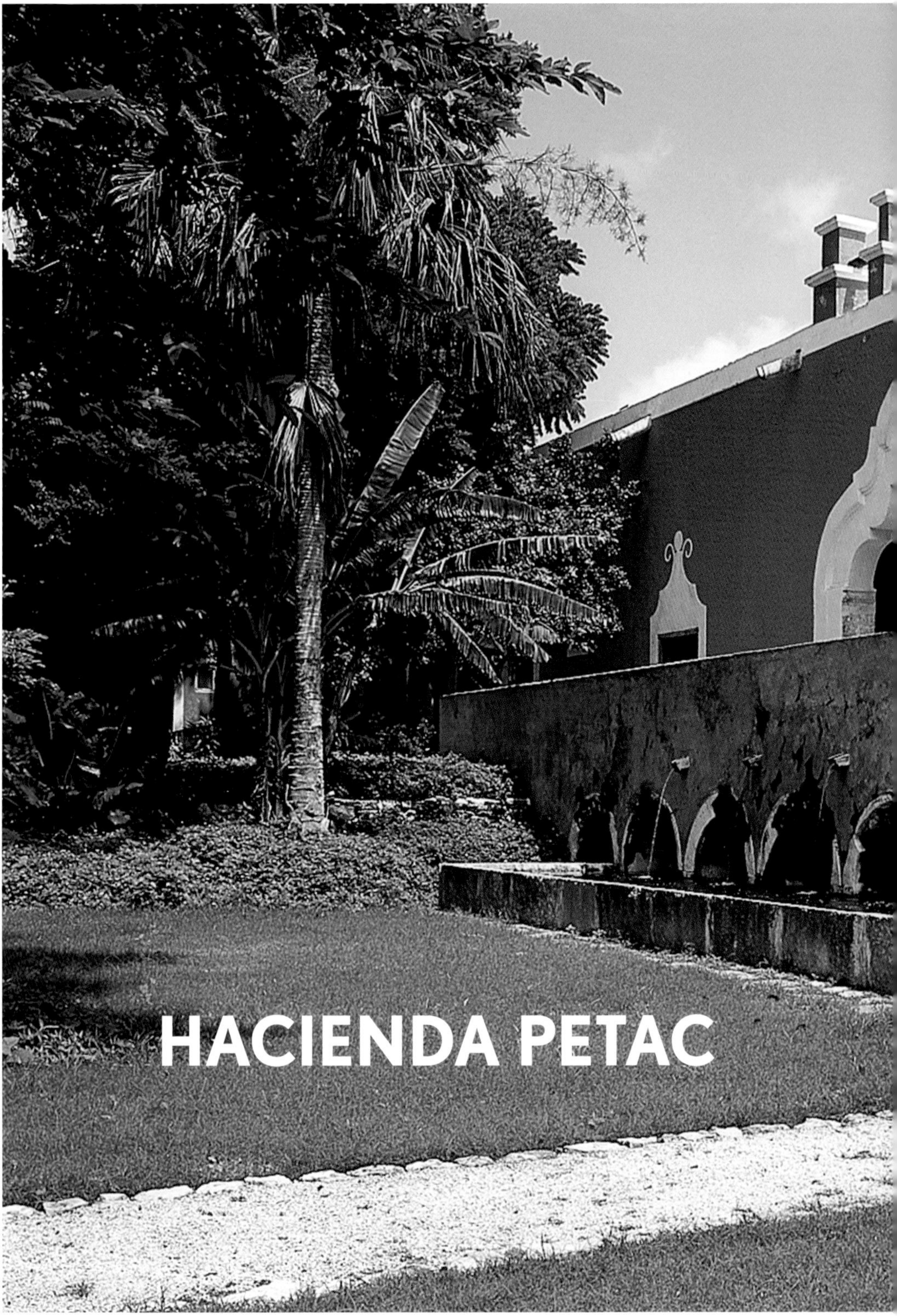
HACIENDA PETAC

HACIENDA PETAC

DEV & CHUCK STERN
YUCATÁN

The Mayans made their mark on the Yucatán peninsula over more than four thousand years. And today the pyramids of Uxmal, Chichén Itzá and Tulum stand as a testimony to their unique culture, which fell into decline after the arrival of the conquistadors, and almost disappeared from the face of the earth altogether. The Mayans, a fiercely proud race, were reduced to slavery and set to work building the main colonial towns. They were also employed at the haciendas processing sisal, a fibre from the henequen (a native Mexican plant). In the early 20th-century, synthetic fibres replaced this "green gold" and, like the Mayan temples, the haciendas crumbled into oblivion, most of them standing as ruins today. Fortunately, Texan couple Dev and Chuck Stern stepped in to save Hacienda Petac, a splendid residence located in Petac, a pleasant drive from the town of Mérida. With the help of architect Salvador Reyes Rios, the Sterns restored Hacienda Petac to its former glory. Today the hacienda is run as a luxury guesthouse, its intimate atmosphere, home comforts and cuisine and its Moorish beauty leaving a lasting impression on all who stay here.

Über 4000 Jahre lang haben die Mayas die Halbinsel Yucatán geprägt. Noch heute zeugen die Pyramiden von Uxmal, Chichén Itzá und Tulum von einer unerreichten Kultur, die nach dem Eintreffen der Conquistadores ihren Niedergang erlebte und beinahe für immer verschwunden wäre. Als Sklaven wirkten die stolzen Mayas am Bau der Kolonialstädte mit und verarbeiteten auf den großen Haciendas Sisal, eine Faser, die vom so genannten Hennequen (der Silberagave) stammt. Zu Beginn des 20. Jahrhunderts lösten Synthetikfasern das „grüne Gold" ab, wodurch die Haciendas, wie schon zuvor die Maya-Tempel, dem Untergang geweiht waren und heute oftmals in Trümmern liegen. Diese beeindruckende Hacienda, die von der Stadt Mérida bequem zu erreichen ist, wurde im letzten Augenblick von dem texanischen Paar Dev und Chuck Stern gerettet. Der Architekt Salvador Reyes Rios verhalf ihr wieder zu ihrem einstigen Glanz. Heute stellen Bewirtung, Komfort, Gastronomie und die von maurischen Stilelementen geprägte Schönheit des Bauwerks auch anspruchsvollste Gäste zufrieden.

Pendant plus de quatre mille ans, les Mayas ont marqué de leur présence la péninsule du Yucatán. De nos jours, les pyramides d'Uxmal, de Chichén Itzá et de Tulum témoignent d'une culture inégalée qui connut son déclin après l'arrivée des conquistadors et qui faillit ensuite disparaître à tout jamais. Devenus esclaves, les fiers Mayas ont participé à la construction des grandes villes coloniales et ont travaillé le sisal, une fibre issue du « hennequen » (une variété d'agave) dans les grandes haciendas. Au début du 20e siècle, la fibre synthétique a supplanté « l'or vert » et, à l'instar des temples mayas, les haciendas ont été condamnées au déclin et souvent ne sont plus que ruines. Sauvée in extremis par Dev et Chuck Stern, un couple texan, la magnifique Hacienda Petac à Petac, située à une distance agréable de la ville de Mérida, a retrouvé sa splendeur d'antan avec l'aide de l'architecte Salvador Reyes Rios. Aujourd'hui, l'accueil, le confort, la gastronomie et la beauté mauresque des lieux satisfont les hôtes les plus exigeants et leur laissent un souvenir inoubliable.

PP. 380–381 A garden path winds across the immaculately kept lawn, leading to the terrace, the antique trough and the "master's house", where the plantation owner once lived. • Über den gepflegten Rasen führt ein Weg zur Terrasse, zur alten Tränke und zum Haus des Eigentümers, in dem einst der Großgrundbesitzer wohnte. • Un chemin tracé dans le gazon très soigné mène à l'abreuvoir, à la terrasse et à la maison du patron, où logeait jadis le propriétaire.

P. 383 The hacienda has been magnificently restored. Visitors can escape the blaze of the midday sun in one of the cool, shady patios in the entrance hall. • Die Hacienda ist meisterhaft restauriert. In einem der Patios im Eingangsbereich kann man sich in der Kühle und im gedämpften Licht entspannen. • L'hacienda a été magistralement restaurée. Dans l'un des patios de l'entrée, les visiteurs peuvent se détendre dans la fraîcheur et la lumière tamisée.

PP. 384–385 Traces of Andalusian architecture are evident in the patio's stunning Moorish arches. • Der mit maurischem Bogenwerk versehene Patio verrät den Einfluss andalusischer Architektur. • Le patio agrémenté d'arches mauresques trahit l'influence de l'architecture andalouse.

↑ The hammocks hung by the hacienda pool beckon with promises of siestas and sweet afternoon dreams. • Die am Swimmingpool der Hacienda angebrachten Hängematten laden zum Ausruhen ein. • Les hamacs suspendus près de la piscine de l'hacienda invitent au doux repos.

→ The architect has made a feature of the passageway leading to the old machine room, adding an ornamental fountain and symmetrical rows of palm trees. • Den Durchgang zu der ehemaligen Maschinenhalle hat der Architekt mit einem Zierspringbrunnen und symmetrisch angeordneten Palmen gestaltet. • L'architecte a enrichi l'ancien passage menant à la salle des machines d'une fontaine-bassin ornementale et de palmiers plantés d'une manière symétrique.

PP. 388–389 Centuries on, the hacienda's old stone reservoir has been converted into a swimming pool. • Die alte Wasserzisterne wird heute als Schwimmbecken sehr geschätzt. • L'ancien réservoir d'eau est devenu une piscine très appréciée.

↑ In the bathrooms natural materials were favoured. • Im Badezimmer wurden natürliche Materialien bevorzugt. • Dans les salles de bains dominent les matériaux naturels.

→ A bedroom is decorated with traditional diamond tiling and twin four-poster beds draped in mosquito nets. • Eines der Zimmer hat rautenförmige Bodenfliesen, dazu zwei ganz identische Betten mit Moskitonetzen. • Une des chambres est agrémentée d'un dallage en losanges et de lits jumeaux à colonnes coiffés de moustiquaires.

PP. 392–393 The hammocks hanging in the the dining room bear witness to the fact that in the olden days any room in the house could function as a dormitory at any hour of the day. • Die Hängematten im Esszimmer weisen darauf hin, dass einst jeder Raum zu jeder Tageszeit in ein Schlafzimmer umfunktioniert werden konnte. • Dans la salle à manger, la présence des hamacs prouve qu'autrefois chaque pièce pouvait être transformée en dortoir à tout moment de la journée.

← The Hacienda Petac bathrooms are equipped with contemporary suites and lighting and the result is an ensemble outstanding for its purity of line. • Die Bäder der Hacienda Petac sind mit zeitgenössischen Möbeln und Leuchten ausgestattet. Herausgekommen ist dabei ein Ambiente, das durch die Klarheit seiner Linien besticht. • Les salles de bain de la Hacienda Petac sont équipées avec un mobilier et des luminaires contemporains et le résultat est un ensemble qui excelle par la pureté de ses lignes.

↑ A Mexican nosegay adds a spray of colour to a bathroom alcove. • Die Blume in der Wandnische bringt zusätzlich Farbe ins Badezimmer. • Dans une des salles de bains, un petit bouquet charmant dans une niche.

↑ → The mirror and the exquisite restoration work on the ancient chapel are a testimony to the beauty of Mexican handicraft. • Der Spiegel und die mustergültige Restaurierung der alten Kapelle zeugen von der Qualität mexikanischen Kunsthandwerks. • Le miroir et la restauration exemplaire de l'ancienne chapelle témoignent de la qualité indéniable de l'artisanat mexicain.

INRI

A TRADITIONAL MAYAN HOUSE

A TRADITIONAL MAYAN HOUSE

HACIENDA YAXCOPOIL
YUCATÁN

Traditional Mayan houses are a frequent sight when travelling through Yucatán. Dotted along country roads beside their more imposing neighbours, the haciendas, many of these houses are centuries old. Built out of stone debris covered in plaster, with their original thatched roofs often replaced by corrugated iron, these modest dwellings offer as little comfort as in bygone days. And yet extreme poverty and harsh living conditions have not destroyed their beauty. The families who live here on simple mud floors possess nothing more than a hammock, a few pieces of furniture and a handful of kitchen utensils. Rooms are lit by neon light and house a fridge and a simple home altar decorated with religious icons, candles and a tiny pile of personal mementoes for prayer and communication with their dead. These ancestors worked for a pittance at the local haciendas, their children and pet dogs their only assets in life. These Mayan houses will doubtless be standing for many more years to come, housing future generations of rural workers.

Wenn man Yucatán bereist, gewöhnt man sich rasch an die Maya-Häuser, die man an den Feldwegen nahe der imposanten Haciendas zu sehen bekommt. Die mitunter jahrhundertealten Gebäude, errichtet aus mit Gips verputzten Steinbrocken und vielfach mit Wellblech und nicht mehr mit Stroh gedeckt, sind heute wie damals wenig komfortabel. Sie bieten Familien Unterkunft, die sich trotz äußerster Armut und schwieriger Lebensbedingungen den Sinn für das Schöne bewahrt haben. Der Boden besteht aus fest gestampfter Erde, und die Bewohner begnügen sich mit ein paar Möbelstücken, einer Hängematte und dem einen oder anderen Kochutensil. Viel Wert hingegen legen sie darauf, dass es Neonlicht gibt, einen Kühlschrank und einen Hausaltar. Hier stehen Andachtsbilder, Kerzen und eine Vielzahl persönlicher Erinnerungsstücke, um zu beten und mit den Verstorbenen, die ihnen am Herzen liegen, in Verbindung zu bleiben. Schon ihre Vorfahren haben gegen mageren Lohn auf den Haciendas gearbeitet, Kinder und Hunde waren ihr ganzer Reichtum. Und wahrscheinlich werden die Maya-Häuser auf dieselbe Weise auch künftige Generationen beherbergen.

En parcourant le Yucatán, on s'habitue vite à contempler les maisons mayas disposées le long des chemins de campagne à proximité des imposantes haciendas. Parfois âgées de plusieurs siècles et édifiées avec des débris de pierres recouverts de plâtre, le chaume du toit souvent remplacé par la tôle ondulée, aussi peu confortables qu'autrefois, elles offrent un refuge à des familles dont l'extrême pauvreté et les conditions de vie difficiles n'affectent pas le sens du beau. Leurs habitants qui foulent un sol en terre battue, se contentent de quelques meubles, d'un hamac et de quelques ustensiles de cuisine, insistent sur la présence d'un éclairage au néon, d'un réfrigérateur et d'un autel domestique où les images pieuses, quelques bougies et un amoncellement de souvenirs sentimentaux leur permettent de prier et de communiquer avec leurs chers disparus. Leurs ancêtres ont travaillé pour un maigre salaire dans les haciendas, n'ayant pour toute richesse que leurs enfants et leurs chiens. Les maisons mayas continueront sans doute à abriter ainsi les générations à venir.

PP. 398–399 These traditional Mayan houses are a frequent sight when travelling through Yucatán. The simple stone abodes house rural workers and their families. • In Yucatán gibt es zahlreiche traditionelle Häuser. Nach wie vor leben darin die ärmsten Familien. • Les maisons traditionnelles sont nombreuses au Yucatán. Elles continuent d'héberger les familles les plus modestes.

P. 401 This simple thatch-roofed house on the Yaxcopoil estate looks much as it did in centuries past. • Der bescheidene Bau mit dem Strohdach, der zum Anwesen Yaxcopoil gehört, hat sein ursprüngliches Aussehen behalten. • Appartenant au domaine de Yaxcopoil, la demeure modeste au toit de chaume a gardé son aspect d'origine.

↑ Whitewashed walls and basic mud floors, this humble abode is a far cry from the luxury of the hacienda next door. • Mit Kalk geweißte Mauern und gestampfte Erde: keine Spur vom Luxus der angrenzenden Hacienda. • Murs blanchis à la chaux et terre battue. Rien à voir avec le luxe de l'hacienda adjacente.

→ and PP. 404–405 All Mayan houses are equipped with the traditional hammock and a home altar dedicated to the saints and the "Holy Virgin of Guadalupe". • Kein Maya-Haus ohne Hängematte und ohne einen kleinen Altar, der den Heiligen und der Jungfrau von Guadalupe geweiht ist. • Pas de maison maya sans hamac et sans petit autel consacré aux saints et à la Vierge de Guadalupe.

comex
aero comex
GRATIS !
160g

TITANIC
NBK
NBK
NBK

A CONVERTED MAYAN HOUSE

A CONVERTED MAYAN HOUSE

HACIENDA SAN JOSÉ
CACALCHÉN

A tragic destiny befell Yucatán's haciendas when production of the "green gold" (sisal) practically died out in the region. Occasionally the vestiges of what were once veritable palaces can be glimpsed through the Moorish arches of an antique portal. But many of these magnificent dwellings have long since crumbled into ruin. Not so the Hacienda San José, which stands as proudly as ever on the road between Mérida and Tekantó. Recently restored to its past glory by Starwood Hotels & Resorts, the hacienda is now the height of 21st-century comfort and sophistication. Guests, who are attracted by San José's history and its breathtaking location, also appreciate the atmosphere of calm and well-being that reigns here. Those seeking an original place to stay, secluded from prying eyes, will adore the old Mayan house, which stands, according to hacienda tradition, in the shadow of the "casa del duegno". The house has been superbly restored by the architect Salvador Reyes Rios, who has managed to transform the former plantation workers' quarters into a luxurious modern guesthouse.

Die Haciendas in Yucatán ereilte ein trauriges Schicksal, als die Produktion des „grünen Goldes", des Sisals, praktisch eingestellt wurde. Viele dieser großartigen Bauwerke liegen in Trümmern. Hier und da erblickt der Besucher hinter einem Portal mit maurischem Bogenwerk die verwitterten Überreste ehemals palastartiger Bauten. Umso erstaunter und erfreuter ist man beim Anblick der Hacienda San José, die an der Straße zwischen Mérida und Tekantó liegt und in ihrer einstigen Schönheit wieder errichtet wurde. Nach der Restaurierung durch Starwood Hotels & Resorts sieht das Gebäude, mit raffiniertestem Komfort ausgestattet, dem 21. Jahrhundert entgegen. Die Gäste wissen es zu schätzen, denn bei aller Faszination für die Vergangenheit und für die Schönheit der Räumlichkeiten suchen sie dort Ruhe und auch Komfort. Für Besucher, die die Originalität abseits neugieriger Blicke bevorzugen, wurde ein altes Maya-Haus restauriert, das traditionsgemäß im Schatten der „Casa del Dueño" stand. Und dem Architekten Salvador Reyes Rios ist es gelungen, eine bescheidene Arbeiterbehausung in einen luxuriösen und modernen Aufenthaltsort zu verwandeln.

Les haciendas du Yucatán ont connu un triste sort quand la production de l' « or vert » a quasiment cessé. Nombre de ces bâtiments grandioses sont tombés en ruines. Ici et là, au-delà d'un portail orné d'arches mauresques, le visiteur distingue les vestiges rongés de ce qui fut autrefois un véritable palais. Dans le cas de la Hacienda San José, située sur la route qui relie Mérida à Tekantó, le regard étonné et ravi s'attarde sur une demeure qui vient de retrouver sa beauté d'antan. Restaurée par les Starwood Hotels & Resorts, la construction fait son entrée dans le 21e siècle dotée du confort le plus sophistiqué. Ce qu'apprécient les hôtes qui, bien qu'attirés par le passé et la beauté des lieux, y cherchent aussi la paix et le bien-être. Pour séduire ceux qui recherchent l'originalité loin des regards curieux, une ancienne maison maya située, comme le veut la tradition, à l'ombre de la « casa del duegno » a été confiée aux soins de l'architecte Salvador Reyes Rios qui a réussi à transformer une pauvre habitation ouvrière en demeure luxueuse et moderne.

PP. 406–407 The gnarled roots of an ancient tree in the park snake across the grass like tentacles. • Wie Tentakel sehen die gewundenen Wurzeln eines Baumes im Park aus. • Dans le parc, les racines tortueuses d'un arbre ressemblent à des tentacules.

P. 409 The house is reached via a path that winds its way through a forest of dense green foliage. • Der Weg zum Haus schlängelt sich durch eine dichte Vegetation. • Le chemin qui mène à la maison serpente sous la végétation touffue.

← In the Hacienda San José, architect Salvador Reyes Rios set a large round bathtub into the middle of a private courtyard; the inhabitants can take their baths in the open air in the knowledge that they cannot be overlooked. • Mitten in einem kleinen Hof der Hacienda San José hat Salvador Reyes Rios eine große, runde Badewanne eingebaut. So können die Bewohner ihr Bad unter freiem Himmel nehmen und sind gleichzeitig vor neugierigen Blicken geschützt. • Dans la Hacienda San José l'architecte Salvador Reyes Rios a installé une grande baignoire ronde au beau milieu d'une cour privative. Elle permet aux habitants de se baigner à ciel ouvert et de rester à l'abri des regards curieux.

↑ In one of the corridors, the windows are fitted with louvre blinds as a protection from the sun. • Die Fenster eines der Flure sind zum Schutz vor der Sonne mit Jalousien-Rollläden ausgestattet. • Dans un des corridors, les fenêtres sont équipées avec des volets à jalousies pour protéger les hôtes du soleil.

P. 412 Everything has been arranged for maximum comfort and well-being. • Alles ist auf Bequemlichkeit und Wohlbefinden der Gäste ausgerichtet. Nur ein paar Schritte sind es vom großzügig bemessenen Divan zur Freiluftbadewanne. • Tout est prévu pour le confort et le bien-être des hôtes. Quelques pas seulement séparent le divan aux proportions généreuses de la baignoire en plein air.

P. 413 Under the cool awning of the patio, guests can choose to linger over breakfast or while away the hours in a hammock. • Unter dem Wetterdach des Patios können die Gäste ein Frühstück einnehmen oder auch sich in einer Hängematte ausruhen. • Les hôtes peuvent prendre leur petit-déjeuner ou se reposer dans un hamac sous l'auvent du patio.

PP. 414–415 This shady retreat is built of natural materials such as wood and bamboo. • Mit den Naturbaustoffen Holz und Bambus wurde ein Schatten spendender Sonnenschutz errichtet. • Cet abri frais et ombragé est construit en matériaux naturels, bois et bambou.

↑ An impressive king-size bed is suspended from the ceiling on thick hemp ropes. This luxury cradle is guaranteed to rock you sweetly to sleep. • Das stabile Kingsize-Bett ist mit starken Hanfseilen in der Decke verankert. Das sanfte Wiegen wirkt schlaffördernd. • Le robuste lit « king size » est suspendu au plafond par de grosses cordes de chanvre. Le doux bercement est propice au sommeil.

→ Salvador Reyes Rios has avoided the pitfalls of "faux rustique" in the hacienda interiors, preferring pure, clean lines and minimalist décor. The bathroom is a striking example of understated design. • Der Versuchung „vermeintlicher Rustikalität" hat der Architekt widerstanden. Die einfachen Formen und die sachliche Gestaltung des Badezimmers lassen seine Neigung zum Minimalismus erkennen. • L'architecte a su rester sourd aux sirènes du « faux rustique ». La simplicité des formes et la décoration dépouillée de la salle de bains montrent son penchant pour le minimalisme.

AMANSALA ECO CHIC RESORT

AMANSALA ECO CHIC RESORT

TULUM

Amansala means "peaceful water" and in this solar-powered resort right beside the sea the guest is permitted to calmly select from the numerous activities on offer. Power Yoga perhaps, or maybe you'd prefer relaxing Restorative Yoga, a day trip on a bike, a sightseeing tour of the Mayan ruins, a kayak tour or a treatment with Mayan clay. You'll begin the day with a brisk power walk, and then after yoga, swimming, massages and another march, after tasty grilled fish and a fresh pineapple juice, sink into the distinctly non-rustic Frette linen under the mosquito net in your little hut. If need be you can still drink one of the best margaritas in the world on the veranda of the hippy-chic little wooden houses. In the candle-light, no one will see you.

Amansala bedeutet „friedliches Wasser", und in diesem solarbetriebenen Resort direkt am Meer dürfen Gäste in aller Ruhe entscheiden, welches der vielen Angebote sie wahrnehmen möchten. Power-Yoga oder lieber Entspannungs-Yoga, Ausflüge mit dem Fahrrad, eine Besichtigung der Maya-Ruinen, eine Kajaktour oder eine Behandlung mit Maya-Tonerde? Beginnen wird man den Tag zum Beispiel mit einem Power-Walk, um dann nach Yoga, Schwimmen, Massagen und erneutem Marsch, nach würzig gegrilltem Fisch und einem frischen Ananassaft in seiner kleinen Hütte unter das Moskitonetz in die völlig unbäuerlichen Frette-Laken zu sinken. Wenn's sein muss, kann man davor noch auf der Veranda der schicken Hippie-Holzhäuschen eine der besten Margaritas der Welt trinken. Bei Kerzenlicht sieht das keiner so genau.

Amansala signifie « eau paisible », et dans ce site en bordure de mer, alimenté à l'énergie solaire, le client peut choisir en toute quiétude ce qu'il aimerait faire parmi les nombreux programmes qui lui sont proposés. Yoga dynamique ou plutôt yoga de relaxation, randonnées à vélo, visite des sites mayas, tour en kayak ou traitement à base d'argile maya ? On commence la journée par une marche soutenue, et après le yoga, la nage, les massages, une nouvelle marche, après avoir dégusté un poisson grillé aux épices et un jus d'ananas frais, on se laisse tomber dans des draps de lin griffés Frette sous la moustiquaire de sa petite hutte. Au besoin, on peut toujours boire une des meilleures Margaritas du monde sur la véranda des jolies maisonnettes de bois de style hippie. À la lueur des bougies, personne n'y regarde de si près.

PP. 418–419 In the paradise of the Amansal Eco Resort, the individual houses are constructed from natural materials and every one of them is different. Surrounded by a dense, protective screen formed of a myriad of palms, they line the beach like a fata morgana and offer a superlative view of the sea. • Die individuellen Häuser des paradiesischen Amansala Eco Resort sind aus natürlichen Materialien erbaut, und jedes sieht anders aus. Umgeben von einem dichten und schützenden Wall aus einer Vielzahl von Palmen, stehen sie am Strand aufgereiht wie eine überwältigende Fata Morgana und bieten einen unverbaubaren Blick aufs Meer. • Dans le paradisiaque Amansala Eco Resort, les maisons individuelles sont construites avec des matériaux naturels et elles ont chacune un aspect différent. Entourées par l'écran dense et protecteur d'une multitude de palmiers, elles s'alignent telle une hallucinante fata morgana le long de la plage et offrent une vue imprenable sur la mer.

P. 421 How lovely to retreat to this hut with its witch's-hat roof for a siesta in the cool and calm of its shade. • Es tut gut, sich für eine Siesta in diese Hütte mit dem spitz zulaufenden Dach zurückzuziehen und sich für einen Moment in der Ruhe und Kühle zu entspannen. • Dans cette hutte au toit pointu, il fait bon se retirer le temps d'une sieste et profiter d'un moment de détente dans le calme et la fraîcheur.

PP. 422–423 Far from the noise and "rat race" of daily life in the big city, Amansala stands before the perfect, blue sea like a metaphor for earthly paradise. • Weit entfernt von jedem Lärm und von der Hektik des Alltags der großen Städte steht das Amansala am Rande eines in allen erdenklichen Blautönen leuchtenden Meeres und wird zum Synonym vom Paradies auf Erden. • Loin du bruit et loin du « rat race » de la vie quotidienne dans les grandes villes, l'Amansala se dresse face à une mer bleue à souhait et devient synonyme de paradis terrestre.

← A few cushions and a table on the fine sand of the beach. The very definition of happiness: what more could anyone need? • Ein paar Kissen und ein direkt auf den feinen Sand eines Strands gesetztes Tischchen – was braucht es mehr zum Glück? • Quelques coussins et une table posée à même le sable fin sur une plage : Que faut-il de plus pour être heureux ?

↓ This Mayan-style house, despite its simplicity, offers guests the luxury of a covered terrace on pilotis, with a chaise longue and hammock close by. • Dieses schlichte Häuschen im Maya-Stil bietet den Gästen den Luxus einer mit Pfeilern gestützten überdachten Terrasse, dazu eine Liege und in Reichweite eine Hängematte. • Cette maison de type maya d'une grande simplicité offre à ses hôtes le luxe d'une terrasse couverte sur pilotis, avec une chaise longue et un hamac à portée de main.

PP. 426–427 If you have to be shipwrecked, what more alluring shoreline could there be than this – provided that your credit card has survived the wreck. • Welch ein Paradies für den an diesen Ufern gestrandeten Schiffbrüchigen, sofern er außer seiner Yacht nicht auch noch seine Kreditkarte verloren hat. • Quel paradis pour le naufragé qui, rejeté sur cette berge, n'a pas perdu ses cartes de crédit avec son yacht.

← Under the Palapa with its many openings, soft, luxurious beds stand beneath diaphanous mosquito nets. The sleep of the guests is soothed by the gentle breezes and the rhythmic beating of the waves. • Unter dem von Palmblättern gedeckten Dach der für Licht und Luft offenen Unterkunft entdeckt man behagliche, mit durchsichtigen Moskitonetzen ausgestattete Betten. In der Nacht werden die Gäste von einer sanften Brise und dem beruhigenden Rauschen der Wellen in den Schlaf gewiegt. • Sous la Palapa ouverte aux éléments, on découvre des lits douillets équipés de moustiquaires diaphanes. La nuit, les hôtes sont bercés par une douce brise et par le bruit apaisant des vagues.

↑ Far from the sophistication of so-called "luxury hotels", the Amansala offers its guest the sole true luxury: calm and relaxation. • Weit entfernt vom ausgeklügelten Komfort edler Luxushotels bietet das Amansala seinen Gästen den einzigartigen und wahren Luxus von Ruhe und Entspannung. • Loin de la sophistication des hôtels dit « de grand luxe », le Amansala offre à ses hôtes l'unique et véritable luxe du calme et de la détente.

Casa Luis Barragán: pp. 10–23, Barbara and René Stoeltie **A Converted Chapel**: pp. 24–37, Barbara and René Stoeltie **Condesa DF**: pp. 38–55, photos supplied by the hotel (Undine Pröhl, Jorge Bustos) **Paloma & Javier Senosiain House**: pp. 56–71, Heiner Orth **Casa de Léon**: pp. 72–85, Barbara and René Stoeltie **Casa de la Torre**: pp. 86–103, Barbara and René Stoeltie **Victor Manuel Contreras**: pp. 104–115, Barbara and René Stoeltie **A Village House**: pp. 116–131, Barbara and René Stoeltie **Arango Residence**: pp. 132–143, Thomas Loof **Villa Tigre del Mar**: pp. 144–159, Barbara and René Stoeltie **Villa Sol de Oriente**: pp. 160–171, Barbara and René Stoeltie **Casi Casa**: pp. 172–187, Barbara and René Stoeltie **Mi Ojo**: pp. 188–199, Barbara and René Stoeltie **Casa Dos Estrellas**: pp. 200-207, Barbara and René Stoeltie **Playa Rosa - Casitas de las Flores**: pp. 208–217, Barbara and René Stoeltie **Verana**: pp. 218–233, all photos supplied by the hotel (Jae Fineberg) **Verana Day Spa**: pp. 234–251, all photos supplied by the hotel (Jae Fineberg) **Hilltop Villa**: pp. 252–269, William Abranowicz / Art + Commerce **Hotelito Desconocido**: pp. 270–273, Photographs courtesy Hotelito Desconocido **Haramara Retreat**: pp. 274–283, photos supplied by the retreat **Endémico**: pp. 284–293, all photos supplied by the hotel **A Collector's Passion:** pp. 294–301, Barbara and René Stoeltie **John Powell & Josh Ramos**: pp. 302–313, Barbara and René Stoeltie **Salvador Reyes Rios & Josefina Larrain Lagos**: pp. 314–327, Barbara and René Stoeltie **A Palapa House**: pp. 328–337, Barbara and René Stoeltie **Hacienda Xcumpich**: pp. 338–353, Barbara and René Stoeltie **Hacienda Poxila**: pp. 354–365, Barbara and René Stoeltie **Casa Cárdenas**: pp. 366–379, Bruce Buck **Hacienda Petac**: pp. 380–397, Barbara and René Stoeltie **A Traditional Mayan House**: pp. 398–405, Barbara and René Stoeltie **A Converted Mayan House**: pp. 406–417, Barbara and René Stoeltie **Amansala Eco Chic Resort**: pp. 418–429, all photos supplied by the resort

The friendship and generosity of Barbara and Maurizio Berger, Evelyn Lambert and Marieke and Pierre Baumgartner made work on this book an absolute joy. We would also like to extend our heartfelt thanks to Catalina Corcuera Cabezut from the Casa Museo Luis Barragán, Mexico, the Barragán Foundation, Switzerland, Sarah Sloan from the Museo Robert Brady, the management at the Hotel Mahakua in Colima, Salvador Reyes Rios and Josefina Larrain Lagos, Maestro Victor Manuel Contreras, Chuck and Dev Stern and Nancy Lara at the Hacienda Petac. And last but not least, a big thank you to everyone who showed us such hospitality and kindness throughout our stay.

Dank der Großzügigkeit unserer Freunde Barbara und Maurizio Berger, Evelyn Lambert sowie Marieke und Pierre Baumgartner war die Produktion dieses Buches ein reines Vergnügen. Dank gebührt auch Catalina Corcuera Cabezut von der Casa Museo Luis Barragán in Mexiko, der Barragán Foundation in der Schweiz, Sarah Sloan vom Museo Robert Brady, der Direktion des Mahakua Hotels in Colima, Salvador Reyes Rios und Josefina Larrain Lagos, Maestro Victor Manuel Contreras, Chuck und Dev Stern sowie Nancy Lara von der Hacienda Petac, und natürlich all jenen, die uns mit großer Gastfreundschaft Willkommen geheißen haben.

Grâce à l'amitié et à la générosité de Barbara et Maurizio Berger, Evelyn Lambert et Marieke et Pierre Baumgartner la production de ce livre fut un véritable paradis sur terre. Un grand merci également à Catalina Corcuera Cabezut de la Casa Museo Luis Barragán, Mexique, la Barragán Foundation, Suisse, Sarah Sloan du Museo Robert Brady, la direction de l'hôtel Mahakua à Colima, Salvador Reyes Rios et Josefina Larrain Lagos, Maestro Victor Manuel Contreras, Chuck et Dev Stern et Nancy Lara de la Hacienda Petac et à tous ceux qui nous accueillirent avec une gentilesse et une hospitalité sans égales.

Barbara & René Stoeltie

IMPRINT

TEXTS BY
Barbara and René Stoeltie, Christiane Reiter, Max Scharnigg, Kristin Rübesamen, Julia Strauß, Ian Phillips, Allison Arieff, Adrienne Arieff, Deborah Bishop, Irene Ricasio Edwards

ENGLISH TRANSLATION
Julie Street, Pauline Cumbers, Iain Reynolds, Sophie Lovell, Robert Taylor, John Sykes, Karin Jaeger, Chris Miller

GERMAN TRANSLATION
Stefan Barmann, Franca Fritz & Heinrich Koop, Ingrid Hacker-Klier, Christiane Burkhardt, Karin Jaeger, Egbert Baqué

FRENCH TRANSLATION
Thérèse Chatelain-Südkamp, Sabine Boccador, Christèle Jany, Philippe Safavi, Michèle Schreyer, Marie Surgers, Hélène Marin and Arnaud Briand for mot.tiff, Annick Schmidt, Alice Petillot

PAGE 2
This mask embroidered with tiny multi-coloured beads was made by craftsmen in the Oaxaca region.

PAGE 6 and 8
The cactus, a highly decorative and part-edible succulent, is perfectly adapted to the tropics of Mexico.

Hohenzollernring 53, D-50672 Köln
www.taschen.com

Printed in Bosnia-Herzegovina
ISBN 978-3-8365-8845-4